A Living Faith

An Historical and Comparative Study of Quaker Beliefs

Wilmer A. Cooper

Friends United Press
Richmond, Indiana

First edition 1990
   Second printing 1991
   Third printing 1993
   Fourth printing 1997
Second edition 2001

Printed in the United States of America

Design by Shari Pickett Veach

          Library of Congress Cataloging-in-Publication Data

Cooper, Wilmer A. (Wilmer Albert)

  A living faith : historical and comparative study of Quaker beliefs/
  Wilmer A.
  Cooper.— 2nd ed.
       p. cm.
   Includes bibliographical references and indexes.
   ISBN 0-944350-53-4
   1. Society of Friends—Doctrines. I. Title.

BX7731.2 .C66 2000
230'.96—dc21
                    00-053568

Dedication

To Emily and our four children

Contents

Preface

This book was first published in 1990. From the beginning it was hoped that this volume would appeal not only to Friends but also to others who want to know more about the Quakers. It has gone through four printings and continues to be in demand for Quakerism classes whether in Friends schools and colleges, or Quaker study groups in Friends Meetings. This new edition is updated after ten years with some additions, corrections, and suggestions that have come from its readers.

For example, the Quaker tree on page 217 shows the growth and decline of the various branches of Friends throughout the world. The statistics reflect a distinction between membership in the traditional sense and meeting attendees who are active participants but choose not to assume membership. Britain Yearly Meeting, for example, has increased attendees with a decline in memberships. On the other hand, in some of the third world countries, such as East Africa, the membership/attender count is not precise enough to fully show the substantial growth of Kenyan Friends.

At the end of the new this new volume I have added a postscript with further reflections on the content of the book, as well as some additional material.

This work grows out of thirty years of teaching theology and social ethics, with the last ten years concentrated on Quaker studies. The content of the book is the product of a course in Basic Quaker Beliefs offered at Earlham School of Religion. When I began teaching the course, I used "handouts" for the students. This process grew until the handouts became the finished product you hold in your hand. The word "finished" must be qualified, however, because our thought processes and our understanding of religious faith are not likely to remain static. As we learn and grow personally our religious faith and understanding are bound to do the same.

This book attempts to deal systematically and comparatively with Quaker beliefs, starting with the historical background of Quaker beginnings in England three and a half centuries ago and taking into account the substantial changes that have taken place in the intervening years. It is written from a North American Quaker perspective, which in itself represents a very broad spectrum of Quaker faith and practice, and is addressed both to Quaker and non-Quaker readers. It is my hope that this work will help Friends gain a fuller understanding of their Quaker heritage and theological roots, while providing for non-Quakers a comprehensive answer to the questions: "Who are the Quakers?" and "What is Quakerism?"

Quakers have always been prolific writers, recording their reflections in journals, histories, and other documented expressions of spirituality. But very little has been written about Quaker *reflection upon* and *interpretation of* that religious experience, which has to do with faith commitments and beliefs. The most notable exception to this was Robert Barclay's seventeenth-century *Apology For The True Christian Divinity*. Since then, most reflective writings have been woven into

Quaker histories, have appeared in tracts or pamphlets, or have been published in the Quaker periodicals. Since 1957 the Quaker Theological Discussion Group, which publishes *Quaker Religious Thought*, has focused on the task of theological reflection and interpretation.

The study itself makes use of both primary and secondary source material. Because it is a theological work of historical interpretation and not primarily a work of objective historical fact, there has been greater use of secondary sources of interpretation than would ordinarily be acceptable. This is not to say that theologians can do as they please with the facts, whereas historians cannot; yet the truth is that wherever interpretive analysis is undertaken, one never has access to raw objective facts. Duty compels us to achieve as much objectivity as possible, but we can never expect absolute objectivity in either theological or historical analysis.

From an editorial point of view, at times I have referred to both sides of an issue, while at other times I may seem to take sides in order to assert my own point of view. Although fairness and objectivity have been sought, I cannot claim to be free of bias in all instances. This of course leaves room for further questioning and discussion. However, I have made an honest attempt to remain open to competing points of view while dealing with the material with candor and integrity, both in content and presentation.

Readers who place themselves at either end of the Quaker spectrum theologically—either liberals such as Quaker unitarians and universalists or Quaker fundamentalists who hold to extremely conservative interpretations of Christian doctrine—may be disappointed not to find more in the book that reflects their respective points of view. However, neither of these positions represents the mainstream of Quaker faith and practice, and it is from this perspective that the book is written. Anyone familiar with the diversity of Friends in the mainstream will know that this mainstream itself still provides great latitude for differing points of view. It is sometimes said that where two or three Friends are gathered together, the same number of opinions will be expressed. So while there is a commitment to a "normative" position on many issues based on past Quaker experience and practice, hopefully this work will speak to a broad spectrum of Friends.

Although this book itself is primarily theological in nature, Chapter 1 provides a brief history of Friends, including the development of pastoral ministry; Chapter 10, "Quaker Mission, Service and Outreach" is an historical treatment, which tells how Friends have translated their beliefs into action; and Chapter 11, "Quaker Assessment and Future Prospects," speculates on where the Quaker movement seems to be going.

Each chapter concludes with several questions intended for persons who want to use the book for discussion purposes. In preparing for the discussion, it may be necessary to draw on other sources of information besides this book, such as the references given in the bibliography. A Glossary of Terms has been provided to help those not familiar with some of the theological language, along with a tree showing the various branches of the Religious Society of Friends and statistical information indicating the size and extent of Quaker growth and decline throughout the world.

Scripture references in the text are taken from the Revised Standard Version of the Bible, unless otherwise indicated.

The preparation of this book has been an unfolding and revealing experience as both students and instructor have wrestled with these theological issues in order to gain a more comprehensive and coherent understanding of our Quaker faith. Credit is due all who have participated in the process and helped fashion the ideas and beliefs spelled out in the chapters that follow. Others have read the manuscript and offered helpful advice. I especially want to thank Ann Miller, Dorlan Bales and David Falls. I also acknowledge the patience and support of my wife, Emily, through the years of study, teaching and writing required to produce this volume.

Wilmer A. Cooper
September, 2000

Introduction

Because Friends have a genuine fear of thinking or talking about faith apart from experiencing it, they have historically regarded theological interpretations and formulations as suspect. This is a major reason for the Friends' testimony against doctrinal statements or creeds, which they regard as being "out of the life." It is not surprising, then, that they have tended to take a negative attitude toward theologizing of any kind and have seldom attempted to examine and interpret their basic beliefs in an orderly and systematic manner.

But the fact is that no one can escape a certain amount of theological reflection and evaluation. Even "God is love" or "that of God in every one" are theological affirmations. When we emphasize the primacy of our faith as inwardly experienced, it is almost inevitable that we give some interpretation to its meaning. At the same time, we often need to reflect upon the meaning of our faith in order to convey it to others. Whenever we pursue any of these tasks, we are engaged in theological work.

It is sometimes said that Quakerism is not a set of beliefs but a way of life, and this is true. Yet we cannot discern a way of life without examining our basic beliefs. We all have to begin somewhere by affirming some basic commitments, even when it is to deny belief in God or to claim agnosticism. These claims in themselves are theological affirmations, even though negative in form.

It is also said that Quakerism is primarily a method for discerning the truth, though not to the exclusion of belief. This view is best expressed by Howard Brinton:

> Quakerism is primarily a method, just as science is primarily a method. Quakerism includes a certain body of beliefs, as does science, but in both cases these beliefs are accepted because they have been arrived at by experts using the proper method. They can be modified by further use of the same method by which they were arrived at in the first place. The scientific method is directed toward the outer world... [while] the Quaker method differs from the scientific method in that it is dealing with what can neither be measured nor weighed. It is directed to the inner life, the response to moral claims and religious insights. Since Quakerism and science are based primarily on experience, rather than reason or authority, they have nothing to fear from the results of discovery or research.[1]

The following story from one of my students reveals the place of "belief" in Quaker faith. This person found his spiritual home among Friends through an unprogrammed meeting of liberal persuasion and, therefore, the story does not fit everyone's experience; but it does illustrate why Friends need to examine the basic assumptions they bring to the religious experience they claim to have. Whether we are conscious of them or not, our faith assumptions impact our religious life.

I came into the Society of Friends by way of a commitment to pacifism. I was a Christian pacifist at the age of thirteen and still a pacifist during the Viet Nam War, although "too sophisticated to be a Christian." After several years of attending a liberal, university town meeting my wife and I became members. After all, Quakers are *tolerant*, and *you don't have to believe anything at all*. And, perhaps best of all, you can do anything you want. [It] sure spoke to my condition! I needed a good bit of tolerance and scarcely believed anything. Yet I think I had already sensed something deeper in the Quaker experience. I initially came to meeting because of my commitment to peace and other social concerns. I came back, and still attend, because of the experience of Meeting for Worship....I am now (again) Christocentric in my orientation. Having read Fox's Journal and some Quaker history prior to becoming a member of the Society, I recognized that the Quaker tradition was undeniably Christian....[2]

The experience of this young man is typical of the religious wasteland in which many find themselves, while at the same time seeking "a place to stand" in their search for a meaningful faith. That in itself is reason enough for writing a book exploring Quaker beliefs.

When referring to Quaker beliefs it would be altogether appropriate to speak of them as "religious testimonies." The term "testimonies" is usually applied to Quaker social concerns, but undergirding these are basic religious principles. The religious testimonies deal with ultimate issues of life and become the spiritual seedbed out of which specific social concerns grow. Although this book does not couch Quaker beliefs in the form of religious testimonies, the important thing to remember is that from a Quaker perspective, beliefs are grounded in religious experience. Hence, beliefs testify to our inner experience of the Spirit working in our lives. Thinking of our beliefs in this way keeps them alive and fresh and helps to avoid the ossification of our faith.

It is not my intention to declare what "true belief" should be for all Friends; rather, my purpose is to encourage Friends to examine their own beliefs and become aware of their theological assumptions (even when they don't think they have any) and to become more articulate about their beliefs so that they can converse with others about them. When we learn to do this, we can begin to expand our understanding, push back our religious horizons, and grow in our faith commitments.

Early Friends such as George Fox, Robert Barclay, and William Penn believed they were recovering "primitive Christianity" as experienced by the early church and recorded in the New Testament Scriptures. Thus, they regarded biblical revelation as normative. By the same token, it is our assumption that the early Quaker vision is normative for us insofar as we are able to discern it and reconcile it with the continuing revelation of God's Spirit. Early Quakers understood their newfound faith to be universal in character, speaking to the condition of all humanity.

The religious experience of early Friends was dynamic, not static, because it was infused with the Holy Spirit. The Spirit of God can never be controlled or manipulated by our own desires or by the cleverness of our minds. To quote the Gospel of John: "The wind blows where it wills, and you hear the sound of it, but you do not know whence it comes or whither it goes; so it is with every one who is born of the Spirit" (John 3:8). This means we must always be open to new leadings and insights for our faith pilgrimage, and these leadings and insights must always be interpreted and applied within the dynamic framework of Spirit-led lives.

In the course of this book we will be quoting Friends from the seventeenth century up through the present in order to establish what is normative for Friends' faith and practice.[3] By "normative" we mean those beliefs and practices that, through the test of time, have formed a central theme and position in Quaker history. Perhaps the most obvious example would be the Peace Testimony of Friends, which offers a consistency in faith and practice from the beginning, even though at any given time there were those Friends who did not fully support it. Other obvious examples would range all the way from the Friends testimony about the Light of Christ Within to their testimony about truth-telling and the refusal to take oaths. Although not all Friends at all times have faithfully embodied these testimonies, it has always been clear that consistent deviation from them was not only a sign of lack of faithfulness but was often grounds for disciplinary action.

Such a normative means of testing Quaker faith and practice does not suggest that Quakers have always been right or that they have not made some misjudgments. For example, George Fox in the seventeenth century and Lewis Benson in the twentieth century both held that from the time of Constantine until the 1650s the Christian church was apostate, and not until its restitution in the seventeenth century did the "true church" surface again. This seems a preposterous claim to make; it simply will not stand up under the careful scrutiny of church history, in spite of the fact that there is a great deal of evidence in its favor. Surely God did not abandon the church until the time of George Fox, whether or not those who claimed to be God's people responded in faithfulness. Perhaps the church was "in the wilderness" during that time, as Fox claimed, but even through the dark years of the Middle Ages there were those who were faithful to God's call.

Although there have been normative practices of Friends throughout their history, based on the early Quaker vision of the Truth, it is too much to claim that early Quaker faith and practice has to be doggedly and uncritically followed in order to remain faithful to the early Quaker vision. Indeed, Friends have always believed that God's revelation is never a closed book, a belief so well expressed by the seventeenth-century Nonconformist John Robinson: "The Lord has more truth and light yet to break forth from his holy word."[4]

Questions for Discussion

1. Why have Friends traditionally been afraid of creeds?
2. Why do Friends avoid theological reflection and affirmation?
3. Is there an inconsistency between theological reflection and being open to the leading of the Spirit of God?
4. What does the author mean by "normative Quakerism" (e.g., the Friends Peace Testimony)?

CHAPTER 1

A Short History

The Religious Society of Friends had its beginning in England in the middle of the seventeenth century, where George Fox (1624-1691) is credited with being the founder of the movement known in the beginning as "Publishers of Truth" and "Children of the Light." The term "Quaker" was first applied in derision by their adversaries because it was observed that in their ministry they quaked in the power of the Spirit.

Broadly speaking, the Society of Friends arose out of the radical Puritan attempt to purify the Church of England, except that the Quakers wanted to go a step further and purify the Puritans. Beyond this, some believe the Friends were originally influenced by the Spiritual Reformers of the sixteenth and seventeenth centuries, particularly those Christian mystics from the continent of Europe who may have migrated to the Trent River Valley and settled in the vicinity of George Fox's birthplace. Others say that Fox received a direct revelation from God that provided him with a vision of "A Great People to be Gathered" in the power of the Lord. Fox recorded in his *Journal* that in despair over his own search for religious truth and a spiritual home he suddenly discovered that "there is one, even Christ Jesus that can speak to thy condition." And when he heard this inward Teacher, his heart "did leap for joy!"

Even though historians will continue to debate about which historical and cultural factors influenced the beginnings of Quakerism, it is clear that Fox and his followers believed that their convictions arose as an inward religious experience of the Spirit of Christ in their lives. This experience of "the Light of Christ Within" was at the same time a call to Christian perfection — that is, a call to live up to the measure of the Light given each person — which resulted in practical righteousness in living out one's faith. Early Quakers believed they had discovered and were bringing alive the essential witness of first–century Christians, thus prompting William Penn to claim that Quakerism was "primitive Christianity revived."

The movement began in the midst of the English Civil War when there was great turmoil in the religious, economic, and political arenas. It was a time of religious ferment and breaking away from the authority of the established church; it was a time of economic inflation and depression; and it was a time of political revolt against the Stuart monarchy; all of which led British historian Christopher Hill to describe England at that period as "the world turned upside down." Quakerism was a response to these tumultuous events as well as a call to righteous living and integrity in daily life. The result was that the religious testimonies of Friends constantly brought them into disrepute and difficulty with the legal authorities, and they were often persecuted and imprisoned for the sake of conscience.

At the same time, George Fox felt the call of God to proclaim the truth of the Gospel and to carry this message not only throughout the British Isles but to the European continent and to colonial America as well. The "valiant sixty" Quaker ministers went out two by two from

Swarthmoor Hall in northwest England to carry the good news that "Christ had come to teach his people himself," and that the call was not only to hear but to obey the leadings of God's Holy Spirit.

Quakers believed they had discovered religious truth; and because they believed this truth came to them from the Light of Christ Within and from the reading of Scripture, they insisted on religious liberty to practice such faith. Sometimes, however, their commitment to individual leadings of the Spirit resulted in an excessive expression of the Spirit known as "ranterism." This raised serious questions among the Quakers themselves over the proper exercise of religious authority as they understood and practiced it. As a result, in the late 1660s Fox and others began to institute corporate discipline by establishing internal organization of the fledgling Quaker movement. Fox called these structures Gospel Order because he believed that Christ was not only the head but the orderer of the church. At the same time, the Scottish Quaker scholar, Robert Barclay (1648-1690), wrote his famous *Apology for the True Christian Divinity*, which provided a theological framework for Quaker faith and practice.

The Act of Toleration in 1689 began to relax the severe restrictions on Quakers and other dissenters. Also, through the influence of William Penn (1644-1718) and the establishment of the Quaker "Holy Experiment" in Pennsylvania in the New World, Friends began to migrate to places where they could enjoy greater religious freedom and civil liberty. By 1691, the year of Fox's death, the first generation of Quaker minister/leaders began to come to an end, marking the close of the first period of Quaker history.

The Quietistic Period

During the eighteenth century, up until the Great Separations of Friends in America in 1827-28, the earlier Quaker zeal and assertive leadership gave way to a more passive stance by the second and third generation of Friends. Two things account for this. First, greater religious tolerance in England meant that the Friends were subjected to less persecution and imprisonment. Second, the Age of Reason dominated the eighteenth century, and Quakers who believed in following the leading of the Spirit were prone to distrust this new mode of rational self-sufficiency. Friends became less vocal, believing they must not "run ahead of their Guide" in ministry, and the result was long periods of silent waiting rather than the preaching of lengthy sermons that had characterized the earlier period.

Although Friends had turned inward, giving rise to the writing of religious journals such as the great *Journal* of John Woolman (1720-1772), they still engaged in significant work. The Pennsylvania Quaker Colony became an experiment in progressive government, protecting human rights and civil liberties not previously enjoyed by the common people. By mid-century the testimonies of Friends were sharpened as they refused to support the French and Indian War; this in turn finally brought an end to Quaker control of the Pennsylvania legislature in 1756. Friends' consciences also became exercised over the slavery issue as articulated by John Woolman, Anthony Benezet (1713-1784), and others.

These testimonies against war and slavery only added to Friends' ongoing concern for the needs and welfare of the poor, the suffering, and the persecuted. They already had a reputation for fair treatment of native American Indians and had developed philanthropic work in prisons, in care for the insane, and in efforts to offset the ill effects of the Industrial

Revolution on workers and their families. At the same time, Friends were diligent to educate their own children in "all things civil and useful."

Internally, the influence of ministers gave way to the assertive leadership of appointed elders and eventually to appointed overseers of the meeting. For the next century the elders were a powerful force in the Society of Friends. Originally their role was to nurture and support the gift of ministry in their meeting for worship; by the turn of the nineteenth century, however, they had also become concerned about right belief as applied to the "approved" writings and public ministry of Friends. The overseers assumed the responsibility of enforcing acceptable behavior in line with the testimonies and beliefs of Friends. Individuals were disowned if they did not measure up to the standards set by the elders and overseers, who proceeded to build a "hedge" around the Society in order to protect themselves, especially the youth, from the ways of the world. Ironically, a religious body that had set out to protect the liberties of its people in faith and practice ended up setting protective boundaries and restrictive disciplines in order to preserve their religious heritage and the Gospel Truth they felt called to proclaim.

Separations and Evangelical Awakening

By the beginning of the nineteenth century two streams of Quaker faith and practice competed with each other. One was the strong evangelical emphasis of traveling ministers who came from England to America, and the second was the more liberal element influenced by the Enlightenment and the new democratic spirit of the times. While the former leaned more and more toward Scripture as the basis for religious authority, coupled with the interpretive role of the Holy Spirit, the latter emphasized freedom of belief and the religious authority of the Light

Within. In Philadelphia, social, cultural, and economic differences also divided city Friends from country Friends. These tensions led to the sad separations of Orthodox and Hicksite Friends in Philadelphia in 1827 and in New York and Ohio the following year. Many names could be associated with these separations, but the most prominent was Elias Hicks (1748-1830), an elderly Friend who represented a liberating spirit in Quakerism.

A second wave of separations took place largely as a result of the ministry and influence of Joseph John Gurney (1788-1847) of Norwich, England. From the time of his visit to America in 1837- 1840 he continued to have a strong evangelical influence. Although not sympathetic to the liberalism of Hicksite Friends, John Wilbur (1774-1856) from New England began to challenge Gurney both in England and America for his departure from "the ancient beliefs and practices of Friends." This led to the Wilbur-Gurney separations in New England in 1845 and in Ohio in 1854. These separations among Orthodox Friends continued through seven yearly meetings. Wilbur's followers became known as Conservative Friends and represented the "smaller body" of Friends, while the orthodox Gurney Friends represented the "larger body."

By mid-nineteenth century the influence of the revival meetings of the Second Great Awakening of evangelical Christianity began to transform American Quakerism, especially in the Midwest and the Carolinas. Conservative splits from Gurneyite Yearly Meetings took place in Western, Iowa, Kansas, and Canadian Yearly Meetings, and eventually in North Carolina Yearly Meeting in 1904. Philadelphia (Orthodox) and London Yearly Meetings did not participate in this second series of separations, although their great influence sometimes helped to precipitate and/or heal divisions.

Along with the ascendancy of Gurneyite orthodoxy came the adop-

tion of pastoral leadership among Friends and the formation of programmed meetings for worship. Joined with this was the development
of concern for missions to other parts of the world. Missionary societies
were formed, and eventually Quaker missionaries carried the Gospel to
the Far East, the Middle East, Latin America, Africa, and Alaska.

Despite their preoccupation with separations for the purpose of
preserving the purity of their various Quaker identities, throughout the
nineteenth century Friends maintained a strong testimony against
slavery, war, bad conditions in prisons, poor care of the insane, and
injustices to American Indians. Quaker service work during wartime,
which became so prominent in the twentieth century, began to take
shape during the American Civil War and the Franco-Prussian War.
And by the end of the century Friends began to seek ways to overcome
their own disunity. This stirring began with the Richmond (Indiana)
Conference of 1887 and the Manchester (England) Conference of
1895. By 1900 the Hicksite branch of liberal Friends had started
working together through various conferences, culminating in the
formation of Friends General Conference that year. The Gurney
Orthodox yearly meetings continued to hold conference every five years
following the Richmond 1887 Conference, resulting in the formation
of the Five Years Meeting of Friends in 1902, which later became
Friends United Meeting (1966).

The Development of Pastoral Quakerism

By the last third of the nineteenth century internal and external
factors had precipitated a change in Quaker practice that marked a
radical departure from the previous two hundred years—a change that
would dynamically affect the Society's future.[1]

Externally, the American frontier was being criss-crossed by tele-

graph lines and railroad tracks. With better transportation and communication available, Quaker communities were more readily exposed to
new ideas. Juxtaposed was the internal decline of the century-old
quietistic practices, including the heavy-handed discipline of the elders
and overseers. Along with this came the growing influence of English
Quaker evangelicals, especially Joseph John Gurney, as well as the
Wesleyan revival and holiness influence.

The membership of Friends began to decline—for several reasons.
They suffered from the indiscriminate disownment of members for
disciplinary reasons. Their worship and ministry based on silence was
often dull and lifeless, especially for young people. The evangelical
emphasis on biblical authority in preference to the Light of Christ
Within, the study of the Bible in the rapidly developing Sunday school
movement, and doctrinal preaching on atonement, conversion, and
sanctification as essential for salvation and growth in the Christian life
had a vital impact upon Quaker faith and practice on the frontier,
tending to replace the original practices and testimonies of Friends.

Already there was a reform movement afoot within a moderate group
of Friends. At the same time the more revolutionary revival movement,
influenced by Wesley, Finney, and Moody, manifested itself in 1867 at
Bear Creek Meeting in Iowa, Walnut Ridge Meeting in Indiana, and at
Earlham College in Richmond, Indiana. Thus, the decade of the 1870s
marked the rapid spread of revival meetings among Orthodox Friends,
particularly under the leadership of Quaker revivalists such as David
Updegraff, Luke Woodard, John Henry Douglas, Esther Frame, and
Dougan Clark, all of whom had either been converted or influenced by
non-Quaker evangelists. As a result, Quaker historian Thomas Hamm
suggests that Orthodox Friends split into "three mutually antagonistic
factions": The Conservative Wilburites, the moderate reformers, and
the revolutionary revivalists.[2] The Conservatives had already separated

in New England in 1845 and Ohio in 1854 over issues surrounding Gurney, and the revival experience caused further separations in the other Orthodox yearly meetings.

In response to a need for membership growth and better pastoral care for newcomers, many yearly meetings followed the practice of Indiana by setting up "general meetings" for spiritual nurture. Preaching for the purpose of winning new converts took place in these meetings led by revivalist preachers. Inevitably their style of leadership clashed with the renewal methods of more moderate Friends such as Barnabas Hobbs, Charles and Rhoda Coffin, Allen Jay, Timothy and William Nicholson, Joel Bean, and Henry Hartshorne, editor of *Friends Review*. In the 1870s and 1880s, however, the aggressive style of the revivalists dominated as they succeeded in gaining new members. It is estimated that between 1881 and 1889 there were 9,000 new applicants for membership in Indiana Yearly Meeting.[3] As a result, pressure was applied to employ individual pastors to provide care and nurture for these newcomers.

Although various factors set the stage for the development of the pastoral system, it was primarily this need to care for new members that forced its adoption. This, in turn, transformed the worship life of the meetings. A clerical class of leadership gave direction to worship and ministry in place of the corporate "waiting upon the Lord" in silence. The leading roles of elders and overseers were gradually taken over by pastors who disregarded the traditional emphasis on the universal ministry of every person. This style of leadership led to programmed worship, which included Scripture reading, hymn singing, pastoral prayers, and prepared sermons. Insofar as silence prevailed, it simply provided opportunity for personal testimonials and witnessing for Christ. It was claimed that such meetings for worship were held under the direction of the Holy Spirit, although one may suspect that sometimes enthusiastic Quaker preachers abused this practice.

The designation of pastoral ministers began with part-time persons who earned a living some other way; yet the pressure was on to release them for full-time service. Giving oneself completely to the "ministry of the Lord" was preferred, and this led to the question of compensation for ministry, which Friends had heretofore opposed. Pastors were so poorly paid, however, that they were frequently forced to take secular employment to support themselves. Thus, the best qualified pastors often migrated to the larger meetings that could better afford to pay them. So in the long run the issue was not the "paid ministry" but the "poorly paid ministry," which tended to attract less qualified persons.

If Friends were going to have pastors, the next logical consideration was the matter of education. How important was it that they have an education at least equal to that of their congregation, and to what extent did they need special training for ministry and pastoral care? At the 1887 Richmond Conference of Orthodox Friends, a Baltimore delegate, Mary S. Thomas, foresaw the next step:

> Dear Friends, if you let this method [of pastoral ministry] in, and I believe in the bottom of my heart that it has nothing to do with the Society of Friends at all, if you let it into the church you will find a theological seminary at the end of it.[4]

Indeed, Mary Thomas was a prophet. By the end of the nineteenth century special training institutes and Bible departments of study for ministry were offered by many of the Friends colleges. Formal graduate degrees were later offered by Guilford College, beginning in the 1950s, and by the Earlham School of Religion, beginning in 1960. The latter became the first fully accredited Quaker seminary, and recently three other Friends ministerial training programs have been added: Houston

Theological Seminary in Texas, Friends Center at Azusa Pacific University in California, and George Fox Evangelical Seminary in Portland, Oregon.

The question of whether Friends should have pastors and programmed meetings still plagues us. Some unprogrammed Friends regard pastoral Quakerism as a contradiction of terms and therefore "illegitimate." But now that we have had such meetings for one-third of our history, these patterns of worship and ministry are probably here to stay. The important issue is that, whatever form of worship and ministry we adopt, we recover the source and power of that worship and ministry so well modeled for us by George Fox and many of our Quaker forbears.

Twentieth Century Liberalism and Evangelical Reactions

Whereas nineteenth century Friends experienced the dominance of evangelicalism and the development of the pastoral system (except for Hicksite and Conservative Friends), the twentieth century began with a major shift to "liberal" thought and practice. Hicksite Friends through the Friends General Conference began to interact with the emerging Quaker liberalism from the former Gurney Orthodox bodies. Many prominent Friends, especially in England, participated in this new "breaking forth" of liberal Quakerism. Rufus Jones from New England, professor at Haverford College and editor of *The American Friend*, probably best represented and symbolized this new mood on both sides of the Atlantic.

One of the aims of this liberal Quakerism was to emphasize a faith and practice that would speak to the new conditions of the times: the scientific age as represented in the new biology and depth psychology, the historical-critical study of the Bible, and the yearning of youth for a religion of realism and vitality that would not conflict with what they were learning in the classroom and the laboratory. A second aim was to bring Friends closer together in service to the world as an expression of the Quaker testimonies.

Many new Quaker ventures were spawned in the twentieth century to help bring these aims and dreams to fruition: the formation of the American Friends Service Committee in 1917, the Friends World Committee for Consultation in 1937, the Friends Committee on National Legislation in 1943, the growth and development of Quaker schools from the lower grades through college age, the Young Friends movement, the experience of Friends in the CPS Camps for conscientious objectors during World War II, the Faith and Life movement of the 1970s, and many other efforts too numerous to mention.

Early in the twentieth century four yearly meetings that had originally joined the Five Years Meeting of Friends disengaged themselves one by one in a backlash against these liberal Quakers, referred to as "modernists" by fundamentalist and evangelical Friends. By 1947 these four (Oregon, Kansas, Rocky Mountain, and Ohio-Damascus), as well as many individual Friends, began to form what would later become the Evangelical Friends Alliance in 1966 and Evangelical Friends International in 1990.

The Quaker tree in Appendix A provides a graphic view of the various separations and subsequent reunions of Friends that have taken place in North America, while the membership chart in Appendix B gives an overview of where Friends are located in the world today, continent by continent. The new dynamic is that the yearly meetings that have come into being as a result of missions sent out to foreign lands now constitute the fastest growth of Quakers in the world. This is especially true in Kenya, East Africa, Bolivia, and Peru. In isolated places in the U.S., Friends are growing in the traditional yearly meeting areas, especially around college and university campuses, but in many yearly meetings the growth pattern is declining or barely holding its own. In all too many cases there is a consistent pattern of decline in membership.

In spite of its checkered pattern of separations and reunions, along with its respective membership growth and decline, the Religious Society of Friends is still very much alive, and notwithstanding its faults, it continues to be a vital force in the world today. But the collective conscience continues to be bothered by the fact that the Society has never fulfilled George Fox's vision of a "Great People to Be Gathered." Fox envisioned Quakerism ("Primitive Christianity revived") as applicable to persons universally, not just the chosen few. The challenge is to revive that original vision and not let Quakerism be "hidden under a bushel."

CHAPTER 2

Sources of Religious Authority

What is religious truth? What is the will of God? These are the fundamental questions every person of faith must ask. Closely allied with these are the questions: How do we know the truth? and, How does God reveal it to us? The answers lead us to the source of religious authority.[1]

Friends believe they can have a direct and immediate relationship with God as the author of their faith and human existence. Their authority, therefore, is based on what they call *firsthand religious experience*. They are not dependent upon the authority of religious intermediaries, such as priests or ministers, though the experience and counsel of such persons may be sought and found to be useful. Neither are they wholly dependent upon the Scriptures, though they consider the Bible their primary sourcebook of religious truth and guidance.

One's understanding of Quakerism is so dependent upon this fundamental starting point that it is important at the beginning to lay out as carefully as possible the assumptions and methodology of Friends with respect to their particular way of discerning religious truth and the will of God. To examine this method of discernment we will need to look primarily at the Quaker understanding of the Light of Christ Within, to consider its relationship to the Holy Spirit, and to examine the role of Scripture in relationship to both of these sources.

The Light of Christ Within

The Light of Christ Within is the central principle of Friends, although a variety of terms have been applied to this divine principle: the Light Within, Christ Within, Inward Light, Inner Light, Spirit of God, as well as the Holy Spirit, Seed, Measure, and "that of God in everyone." Because Friends have never been precise about theological language, they have often used these terms interchangeably without recognizing the different meanings they might convey.

The metaphor of the Light was so commonly used by George Fox and early Friends that they were referred to as "Children of the Light."[2] The term "light" has a number of biblical sources (e.g., 1 Thess. 5:5 and Eph. 5:8), but for Friends its primary sources were John 1:9 and 8:12. Robert Barclay referred to John 1:9 as "the Quaker text": "That was the true Light, which lighteth every man that cometh into the world" (KJV).[3] George Fox further amplified this:

Now the Lord God hath opened by his invisible power how that every man was enlightened by the divine light of Christ; and I saw it shine through all, and that they that believed in it came out of condemnation and came to the light of the life and became children of it, but they that hated it, and did not believe in it, were condemned by it, though they made a profession of Christ. This I saw in the pure openings of the Light without the help of any man, neither did I then know where to find it in the Scripture; though afterwards, searching the Scripture, I found it. For I saw in that Light and Spirit which was before Scripture was given forth, and which led the holy men of God to give them forth, that all must come to that Spirit, if they would know God, or Christ, or the Scripture aright, which they that gave them forth were led and taught by.[4]

In keeping with the Johannine interpretation, Fox identified the Light with the *Logos*, the pre-existent Christ, and in turn identified the pre-existent Christ with the historic Jesus. Therefore, whatever variation is used, the primary referent is Jesus Christ. Some, in fact, would prefer to use "Christ language" altogether in place of "Light language," believing that it is more faithful to Fox's understanding.

Among the studies of the Light Within, one that is noteworthy is Rachel Hadley King's *George Fox and the Light Within*. She concluded that for Fox the Light was that which shows us evil and that which brings us into unity with God and one another.[5] The first is an ethical emphasis on turning from evil to the good, whereas the second has to do with salvation, which is reconciliation with God and with one another in the community of faith. King writes: "In Fox's thought the one thing essential for salvation is faith in the light, which includes living in the light, which means turning toward the light and away from the evil which the light makes manifest."[6]

Howard Brinton enlarged on this definition when he said that the Light is also the source of *truth*, the source of *power* to act on the knowledge of that truth, and the source of *unity*, wherein as we are obedient to the Light we are brought into unity with God and one another. This is the redemptive process by which we are reconciled with God and all creation.[7]

Early Friends believed that if they waited in the Light and walked in the Light they would be endued with power to overcome sin and moral darkness and come into the Light of the glory of God. This victory over sin and evil constituted a doctrine of perfection: if they responded to the Light of Christ, they would be empowered to live up to the measure of the Light that was given them.

In order to more clearly define the meaning of the Light Within, however, we need to look at some of its distinguishing characteristics.

1. The Light is experienced as the direct and immediate presence of God. Robert Barclay identified our capacity to receive the Light with what he called the Seed of God within, the *vehiculum Dei* (the divine receptacle or conveyor), which by God's grace makes possible the divine-human encounter.[8] Fox frequently used the term "that of God in everyone" to suggest the same meaning.[9] This meaning is prerequisite to understanding the other usages of the term.

2. As already indicated, the Light was identified with Christ by early Friends and was referred to as the Light of Christ Within. It is always *from* God or Christ and therefore is divine in origin. Likewise, it is transcendent in the sense that it stands apart from and beyond our finite existence.

3. The Light was understood by early Friends to be universal. Taking their clue from John 1:9, they maintained that the Light of Christ enlightened "every man," which included believers and nonbelievers alike. Barclay wrote:

> God, who out of his infinite love sent his Son, the Lord Jesus Christ, into the world ... has given a certain day or time of visitation to everyone .... For this purpose God has communicated and given a measure of the light of his own Son, a measure of grace, or a measure of the Spirit to every man.[10]

Both Fox and Barclay held that whether one had heard of the

historical Jesus or not, it was possible to be saved by Christ through the inward work of grace.

4. The Light of Christ was understood to be the Inward Teacher of righteousness. This assumed a dynamic personal connection between oneself and God that allowed one to enter a "hearing and obeying" relationship with God, to use a figure of speech drawn from Lewis Benson, who said:

> The encounter with Christ, the Light, is an encounter with a personal sovereign will that is distinct from our own will. This Light reproves and condemns and calls to repentance. It is experienced as a voice of command that must be heard and obeyed. This is what gave moral certainty and moral strength to the early Quaker community.[11]

Benson has repeatedly pointed out that the essence of Fox's understanding of the Light of Christ is expressed in his oft-repeated phrase, "Christ has come to teach his people himself."[12]

5. The Light Within is not to be identified with or confused with conscience and reason, but both can and need to be illuminated by the Light of Christ.[13] In order to clarify this distinction Barclay compared conscience to a lantern and the Light to a candle that burns within the lantern. Both Fox and Barclay believed conscience and reason were natural capacities that needed to be illuminated by the divine Light of Christ before they could become dependable guides for human action.[14]

6. Response to the Light is also to be discerned in the community of faith. Fox and other early Friends formulated a doctrine of the church that found expression in the concept of the Gospel Order. Christ was not only the Inward Teacher for the individual, but also the one who ordered the fellowship of believers. Here, too, the presence of Christ

was experienced as prophet, priest, king, and divine orderer. A marvelous example of this corporate response was the Friends' Declaration to Charles II in 1661:

> The spirit of Christ, by which we are guided, is not changeable, so as once to command us from a thing evil and again to move unto it; and we do certainly know, and so testify to the world, that the spirit of Christ, [which] leads into all Truth, will never move us to fight and war against any man with outward weapons, neither for the kingdoms of Christ, nor for the kingdoms of this world.[15]

Gospel Order meant decision-making by the group (or the meeting) acting in obedience to Christ. To quote Douglas Gwyn, it is the "Quaker discipline of waiting for the Lord's guidance and teaching which represents a focused effort to be open to divine structuring in the life of the meeting and its members."[16]

Despite the views of Fox, Barclay, and others, Friends have not always agreed on the meaning of the Light Within. In fact, the use of the term—as well as the abandonment of the term or failure to use it— has been a source of division among Friends for several reasons.

First, for many Friends today the seventeenth-century worldview of Robert Barclay is outmoded. Barclay was strongly influenced by the philosophical dualism of Descartes and by Calvin's view of human nature. Based on these assumptions, Barclay understood the Light of Christ not as a part of human nature, but as supernaturally added. In contrast, much modern Quaker thought, especially that which has been influenced by Jungian psychology and process thought, sees the divine image, the Light Within, as an essential aspect of the human unconscious. This would suggest that the religious dimension of the self is part and parcel of the human self, rather than being derived from a source of spiritual reality that transcends humanity. Richard Ullmann has pointed out that whether or not we have clear philosophical and psychological understandings of the relationship of the Light to human nature and to God, how we resolve this issue makes a profound spiritual and existential difference. He writes:

> "That of God" is of *God*, not of man; religious experience is not a soliloquy of man with himself, but a confrontation of man with that which is infinitely greater ... Man does not experience his own presence but that of an overwhelming Other ... It is at least inaccurate to assert that the experience of Christ within meant for early Friends the same thing as divine immanence. For it was an essential part of their religious experience that there was that Other, that outside which *all the same* they discovered so very much within. Religious experience was for them an I-Thou experience....[17]

If the Light Within is no more than ourselves or no more than a level of the unconscious, then it will have little redemptive power; and if the distinction between the divine and human is thereby lost, then the transforming power of the Light will have no effect.

A second problem for Friends is how to relate the Light of Christ Within to the Jesus of history. Quakers have always asserted that they acknowledge only one Christ and have denied the separation of the Christ Within from the Christ of history. They believe that the inward dimension needs to be understood as functioning in and through the outward and historical. This is at the heart of an incarnational understanding of Jesus Christ, or what Quakers would call a sacramental view of the Christ Within and the Christ of history. Instead of polarizing the Christ of faith and experience and the Christ of history, we need to unite them in action. According to Elbert Russell, Friends have tested this relationship by asserting that the leading of the Inward Christ must agree with "the principles of Jesus' teaching and character." Furthermore, they check all supposed leadings or revelations against the recorded spirit and teaching of Jesus.[18] Howard Brinton took this a step further by saying that although Jesus was completely human in that "he was tempted like as we are," he was also divine in that he possessed the Light without measure. And "since the Light Within is God revealing Himself to man, Jesus of Nazareth was God revealing Himself in history."[19]

A third issue is whether the Light Within is sufficient for salvation or whether its efficacy is dependent upon the atoning death of Christ on the cross. Friends have been divided in their interpretation of this question, which also relates to two others: first, whether we have the capacity to save ourselves or whether our human sin is so deep that only through divine intervention can we be reconciled to God; and second, whether the Christ Within is sufficient for our faith or whether the inward and outward are so interdependent that the Christ Within and the Christ of history are indispensable to each other. It is clear from the historical record that early Friends, in keeping with the Puritan tradition of their time, took for granted that the sacrificial death of Christ was essential and that the efficacy of the Light Within was dependent upon it.

Regardless of how we may view this central Quaker principle of the Light of Christ Within—and certainly Friends are not united on this—we must "hold that Christ is present, that he guides and directs, and that his will can be known and obeyed."[20] This is a religious truth we know experientially, not by handed-down authority nor by a forensic act of God that takes place apart from human responsibility and accountability. When we follow the Light of Christ Within there is a conscious obedience to the will of God; and when we disregard the Light of Christ we consciously disobey the will of God. But if we respond affirmatively to the Light of Christ Within it will free us from the bondage of sin and evil and will set us at liberty to be joined together in fulfilling God's will in the world.

Friends and the Holy Spirit[21]

From the beginning the Society of Friends has been a movement of the Holy Spirit. As mentioned earlier, the very name "Quaker" was initially a derogatory term applied because Friends were observed to quake in the power of the Spirit when they appeared in ministry. Empowerment of the Spirit of God and of Christ has been the norm Friends have aspired to emulate throughout their history, although they have not always manifested it in practice. While other religions often speak of a "spirit" as the source of faith and life, the Holy Spirit is a term unique to the Christian faith. By the Holy Spirit we are enabled to discern Jesus Christ as central to the biblical revelation, and it is Jesus Christ who in turn reveals God to us. Friends understand the Holy Spirit to be "the living Christ" whom George Fox and early Quakers discovered and proclaimed in their ministry. Fox frequently declared "the power of the Lord was over all," and he acknowledged a linkage here with his personal discovery that "there is one, even Christ Jesus, that can speak to thy condition." For Fox and early Friends the Holy Spirit was the resurrected Christ who is now present with us. He is not only the promised Counselor referred to by the Gospel of John (14:26) but is also identified with Jesus of the Synoptic Gospels, the incarnate Son of God who lived, taught, suffered, died, and rose again. He is the one who appeared at Pentecost and gave life to the early church (Acts 2). Hence, the Holy Spirit is that which gives life to the church as the community of Christian believers.

But if the Holy Spirit is the Living Christ, in Friends terminology, how does this relate to other terms used to speak of the essentially spiritual relationship of the believer to God through Jesus Christ? To say that Friends have never been very precise about theological language, or very orthodox in their view of the Trinity, provides only a partial answer to how and why they have used a variety of terms to refer to their sense of an immediate relationship to the Divine. The fact is that since the separations of Friends in the nineteenth century there have been two streams of theological thought: the Inward Light Quakers who have emphasized the "Light motif," and the more orthodox and biblically oriented who have emphasized the "Spirit motif." Among evangelical (Gurneyite) Friends in the nineteenth century, Light language was almost completely abandoned in favor of Holy Spirit language. In contrast, the liberal stream of Friends, especially in the Hicksite tradition of the late nineteenth and early twentieth centuries, adopted Light language almost exclusively, with little reference to the Holy Spirit. The tendency has been for the Light–oriented Friends to adopt a more rationalistic form of Quaker thought, whereas the more evangelical Friends have been primarily Spirit–oriented, although they have tended toward their own form of rationalism in their reliance upon doctrinal statements of faith.

Even recognizing these two streams of Quaker thought, Friends from the beginning have used various terms synonymously when referring to the Inward Teacher and Divine Witness in persons. Some have held that the Light, Spirit, Seed, Measure, "that of God in everyone," and Christ Within had a common meaning for early Friends and therefore can be used interchangeably. Others claim that the Light Within and Holy Spirit are not the same. And still others maintain that a distinction needs to be made between the human capacity to receive the Light or the Spirit and the gift of grace experienced in the coming of the Light or the Spirit from God. This is to suggest that the Seed spoken of by Robert Barclay, or "that of God in everyone" spoken of by George Fox, represented the God-given capacity to receive the Light and the Spirit. Such a view recognizes our dependence upon God and acknowledges our human finitude, thus avoiding too much reliance upon our own ingenuity.

It should be noted here that this inward principle, whatever Friends call it, is sometimes identified with the concept of *imago Dei* (image of God) in the Bible, specifically in the creation story of Genesis. However, this relationship seems easier to establish with the Light of Christ Within (which implies a God-given capacity) than it does with the Holy Spirit (which implies the immediate mystical presence of God).

The Holy Spirit as a manifestation of the Living Christ should also be understood as a corporate experience of the body of believers gathered in worship, ministry, and fellowship. When Fox declared that "the power of the Lord was over all," he was also referring to the corporate gathering of those who meet in the presence and power of God and the Holy Spirit. This gathered fellowship then becomes the visible sign of the unity of the church which is drawn together by the Spirit of Christ. Friends claim to carry on their meetings for worship and business in the presence of this unifying Spirit and Light. Thus, a Friends Meeting is intended to be an alive and prophetic fellowship of the Holy Spirit as well as a community of love in action.

Whether we are speaking personally or corporately, the Holy Spirit as the first principle of religion represents a firsthand experience of the living God. In this sense religious knowledge is immediate and direct and not dependent upon the authority of what someone else says. The important thing for George Fox was always, "What canst thou say?" based on one's firsthand knowledge of God. Both Fox and Barclay were so clear about the primacy and immediacy of the Spirit that they declared it to be the basis of religious authority, ahead of Scripture.

If Friends are to keep their roots in the biblical Christian tradition, consistent with their history, then they need to clearly articulate their faith and practice. In pursuit of this, they should take a new look at the Holy Spirit as a way of re-articulating the centrality of the Quaker message and vision. From the beginning Friends have tended to run off into ranterism (religious individualism), unrestrained by corporate discipline in thought and action. The apostle Paul said that "where the Spirit of the Lord is, there is freedom" (2 Cor. 3:17), but that freedom is not license to do as we please in the name of the Lord and the Holy Spirit. Responsible discernment of the Spirit is imperative as we try to determine the will of God.

The Role of Scripture in Religious Authority

Early Friends immersed themselves in the Bible, which was so much a part of their religious culture that its authority was taken for granted. It was said of George Fox that were the Scriptures lost he could reconstruct them from memory. Whether or not this was true, it is clear that he and other Friends were not only familiar with the Bible, but took it seriously as a religious guide for their lives.

Scripture was the touchstone by which their Puritan contemporaries judged "doctrines, religions and opinions." But to this George Fox replied: "Oh no, no, it is not the Scripture…but I told them what it was, namely, the Holy Spirit, by which the holy men of God gave forth the Scripture."[22]

George Boobyer says that to understand the Quaker attitude toward Scripture one has to begin with their view of the Light Within.[23] He notes that in the introduction to Fox's *Journal* William Penn wrote:

They [the Quakers] were directed to the Light of Jesus Christ within them. [This was] their fundamental principle, the corner stone of their fabric, and, to speak eminently and properly, their characteristic or main distinguishing point or principle.[24]

Fox referred to the Light Within as "Christ the inward teacher" who had come to teach his people directly and inwardly. He further said that he "was to direct the people to the Spirit which gave rise to the Scripture." He even claimed that this divine Spirit "is Scripture within thee."[25]

In his *Apology* (Prop. III) Robert Barclay spoke of Scripture as a stream that flows from a fountain, which is the Spirit and is the source of the stream. Using this metaphor to help distinguish between the Scripture and its source, he said that the Scriptures "are only a declaration of the fountain, and not the fountain itself, therefore they are not esteemed the principal ground of all truth and knowledge... [but] they are and may be esteemed a secondary rule, subordinate to the Spirit...."[26]

Friends also believed that the Scriptures were "the words of God" rather than "the Word of God" as the Puritans claimed. Friends believed, as do many contemporary theologians today, that the "Word" was Christ who pre-existed Jesus and was the *Logos* referred to in the Prologue to the *Gospel of John.*[27]

In spite of the fact that Friends regarded Scripture as a secondary rule of faith, they made use of Scripture in their preaching, and Barclay used Scripture freely to "prove" his propositions. He said: "We do look upon them as the only fit outward judge of controversies among Christians...."[28]

Friends also made it clear that to understand the Scriptures and to accept them as authoritative the Holy Spirit must be invoked as their true interpreter, since it was this same Spirit who initially gave the

Scriptures. Fox said: "All must come to that Spirit, if they would know God, or Christ, or the Scriptures aright, which they that gave them forth were led and taught by."[29]

If early Friends differed from their Puritan predecessors by rejecting Scripture as the primary rule of faith, on what grounds did they do so? According to Dorlan Bales, Barclay used four tests to determine this:[30]

1. A primary rule of faith must not depend upon any source other than itself for its authority. Because the Bible depends upon the Spirit as its source, it cannot be a primary source.

2. A primary rule of faith must establish the difference between law and Gospel. The Bible, like the law, is outwardly written and therefore does not qualify as a primary rule, whereas the Gospel is an "inward spiritual law, engraven in the heart" and therefore qualifies as "the law of the Spirit of life."[31]

3. The primary rule of faith must be able to guide the Christian in every situation in life. In broad outline the Bible can tell Christians what they ought to do, but it is the Spirit that gives guidance in specific detail. Moreover, the Bible describes the "marks" of salvation, but it is the Spirit that can assure one of salvation.

4. The primary rule of faith must reach all persons. The Bible cannot do this because not all have knowledge of or access to it (for example, the blind, the insane, children, or people in lands where the Bible has not been taken or translated). Only the Holy Spirit can reach those persons who have not been exposed to the Gospel through the ordinary reading of the Scriptures.

Barclay held that even though, for these reasons, the Bible cannot be relied on as a primary rule of faith, it does play an important role in religious authority for three reasons. (1) The Bible is the main source of inspiration and encouragement to believers. (2) The Bible sets forth the teachings and admonitions of Christ to instruct new persons in the faith.

And (3) the Bible provides us with tests against which the leadings of the Spirit can be judged and verified.

Looking at later periods of Quaker history we find many points of divergence with respect to Friends' understanding of Scripture in relationship to religious authority. When evangelical Christian thought impacted the Society of Friends in the late eighteenth and early nineteenth centuries, a new emphasis was placed on the authority of Scripture as compared with the Light Within. The Holy Spirit was still important for the interpretation of Scripture, but the primacy of the Light Within steadily waned during this period. Extreme evangelical interpretations of this view were held by Isaac Crewdson in England (d. 1840) and Elisha Bates in Ohio (d. 1861), with a more moderate view held by Joseph John Gurney. Both Crewdson and Bates later left the Society of Friends, while Gurney made a lasting impact, especially in America. The net result of this evangelical trend was more emphasis on the letter of Scripture and a stress on the outward work of Christ rather than the inward transformation of the heart by the Spirit of Christ. Also, certain theories of inspiration of the Scriptures were claiming the inerrancy of the Bible. For these Friends, who made up more than half of the Society in the nineteenth century, Scripture replaced the Inward Light as the primary authority for faith and practice.

By the latter part of the same century another attitude toward Scripture developed among a group of Friends in the liberal tradition. The roots of this went back to Elias Hicks and the Great Separations of Friends in 1827-28. Later, from the quietistic side of Quakerism, John Wilbur gave impetus to the development of the Conservative Friends, who emphasized the primacy of the Holy Spirit, though not at the expense of abandoning the Bible. Just as the evangelicals were claiming the inerrancy of the Bible and the liberals were relying almost exclusively upon the Inward Light, the Conservative Wilburites were espousing dependence upon the Holy Spirit informed by Scripture.

These lines of divergence hardened in the late nineteenth and early twentieth centuries. In 1884 the evangelical position was challenged by the publication of *A Reasonable Faith* by three relatively unknown British Friends.[32] The evangelical position, on the other hand, became further solidified by the publication of the *Richmond Declaration of Faith* by an American conference of Orthodox yearly meetings that met in Richmond, Indiana, in 1887. The liberal challenge was further highlighted by the 1895 Manchester Conference in England and by the appearance of several very able liberal Quaker scholars, teachers, and ministers: John Wilhelm Rowntree, Edward Grubb, William Charles Braithwaite, Rendel Harris, John William Graham, and Rufus Jones. These Friends had no intention of downgrading the importance of the Scriptures, but they were committed to keeping alive the historic commitment to the primacy of the Spirit and the Light of Christ Within. Having been schooled in modern biblical and scientific criticism, they proceeded to re-evaluate many of the traditional assumptions about the Bible, intending to derive from the Scriptures and the history of Quaker and Christian thought a relevant message that would speak to the youth of the new scientific age.

These same general divisions regarding the interpretation and authority of Scripture have persisted to this day. Evangelical Friends rely primarily on Scripture coupled with the interpretive role of the Holy Spirit, while liberal Friends rely on the Light Within with occasional support from the Bible. Conservative Friends, though declining in numbers, continue to maintain a balance between the inward authority of the Spirit and the Light Within and a traditional reverence for Scripture.

Questions for Discussion

1. How is the term "religious authority" used in this book?
2. What was the relationship between the Light and Christ in the thinking of George Fox and early Friends?
3. Was knowledge of Jesus Christ essential in early Quakerism in order to be reconciled with God (i.e., salvation)?
4. What was the relationship of the Light to conscience in early Quaker thought?
5. How have Friends related the Light of Christ Within to the Jesus of history?
6. How can the Holy Spirit help Friends express their first-hand religious experience in Christian terms?
7. How can Friends maintain spiritual vitality free from mystical vagueness or spiritual anarchy?
8. How can Friends discern truth from error in the leading of the Holy Spirit?
9. How have Friends regarded the authority of Scripture in relationship to the Light Within and the Holy Spirit?

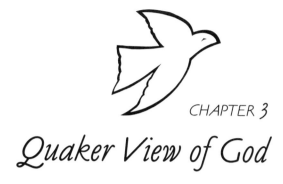

CHAPTER 3

Quaker View of God

Some fifty years ago Rufus M. Jones said, "There is, it must be said in all frankness, no distinctly Quaker conception of God."[1] Although this may overstate the case, the fact is that Quakers are not given to speculation about God. Nevertheless, they do begin with certain basic assumptions about the nature of ultimate reality, or what Paul Tillich called "the ground of our Being." Early Friends clearly took God for granted based on what they believed to be their direct inward experience of God. The phrase that appears more often than any other in the journal of George Fox is "the power of the Lord [or God] is over all," and by this he meant a sense of the personal presence of God as enabler on every occasion and in every situation in life. It didn't seem to occur to him or other Friends to speculate about the nature and attributes of God. It was enough that God was present with them.

In systematic theology it is customary to consider the classic arguments for the existence of God: the *cosmological* argument from first cause; the *teleological* argument from design; and the *ontological* argument from a perfect idea of God, which presupposes existence. But Friends have long maintained that such logical claims can never convince anyone of the existence of God, let alone prove God's existence. Rather, Friends have insisted that to know and claim that reality God must be experienced spiritually within. Thus, Friends have never begun their search for God in the realm of logic, nor in the external world of nature, nor in the far reaches of space and time. For them God is infused Spirit rather than abstract external being.

Early Friends were, however, sufficiently rooted in the Puritan (Calvinist) tradition to have a clear sense of the transcendence of God— that is, the greatness and goodness and majesty of God. Although they knew the inward and immediate presence of God, they understood that God was much more than what they experienced personally. God transcended creation by standing apart from and beyond their immediate awareness of the Divine.

Friends believed that God as spirit was fully disclosed in Scripture, especially in the book of Psalms and in the New Testament writings of Paul and John. A favorite passage in the latter is John 4:24: "God is spirit, and those who worship him must worship him in spirit and truth." Beyond such passages of Scripture, Friends believed that evidence for God was most fully revealed through the person of Jesus. It was through worship, as John 4:24 indicates, that Friends were able to have direct and immediate experience of God by way of what they called "the Christ within." This divine-human encounter is called mystical experience by many Friends. Insofar as there is a gulf between God and ourselves, this immediate experience of God bridges that gap and brings us into the presence of God so that our experience becomes firsthand rather than a secondhand report about God.

The Trinity

In the early years of the Quaker movement William Penn wrote a treatise entitled, *The Sandy Foundations Shaken*, which took issue with the doctrine of the Trinity; as a result, he was imprisoned in the Tower of London. This and other objections led to the common notion, still prevalent, that Friends did not believe in the Trinity. Their main objection was that the Trinity suggested three substances, or three gods, rather than the unity of the Godhead. Friends also held that the Trinity was unbiblical, and Fox's advice was always "to keep to Scripture language, terms, words and doctrine ... in matters of faith, religion, controversy and conversation."[2] The only scriptural reference that seems to substantiate the Trinity is 1 John 5:6 (KJV): "For there are three that bear record in heaven, the Father, the Word, and the Holy Ghost: and these three are one." Apparently this was not considered the final word by early Friends.[3] Also, the authenticity of this text has been questioned by some biblical scholars.

Merely because Friends took issue with traditional formulations of the Trinity in order to preserve the unity of the Godhead, it should not be assumed that they were unitarian in doctrine. Certainly they believed in the divinity of Christ, the uncreated, pre-existent, eternal *Logos* in whom God dwelt in fullness. Their main concern was to emphasize the indwelling power of Christ who was to be known and mediated by the Holy Spirit.

Also, because Friends have always been non-creedal, it is assumed that they have not taken seriously the central doctrines of the Christian faith. To the contrary, most early Friends subscribed to the Christian beliefs embodied in the Apostles' Creed. In *George Fox and the Light Within*, Rachel Hadley King commented on Friends' adherence to these basic Christian beliefs:

In spite of Fox's refusing on principle to accept the Apostles' Creed as an authoritative creed, he nevertheless believed all the clauses of the creed except the one on the resurrection of the body. And in spite of denying the Trinity as unscriptural, he did believe in the Father, Son, and Holy Ghost. In fact, Fox's belief in the light is in some respects a reaffirmation of a belief in the Holy Spirit.[4]

William Penn, in spite of his treatise against the doctrine of the Trinity, said: "Mistake me not, we have never disowned a Father, Word, and Spirit, which are one." What he rejected was "heathenish metaphysics" and "men's inventions" with respect to the Trinity.[5] Other early Friends can be quoted to substantiate their view of the triunity of the Godhead, as well as their orthodox understanding of the Godhead and their exalted view of God.[6] Isaac Penington wrote:

This I believe from my heart, and have infallible demonstrations of; for I know three, and feel three in spirit, even an eternal Father, Son and Holy Spirit, which are but one eternal God . . . Indeed friends, we do know God sensibly and experimentally to be a Father, Word and Spirit, and we worship the Father in the Son by his own Spirit, and here meet with the seal of acceptance with him.[7]

Although seventeenth century Friends often took issue with their Christian and Puritan forebears on matters of faith and practice, it is evident that they had much in common with them doctrinally.

Transcendence and Immanence of God

Fox and Barclay believed that they experienced two levels of reality: the natural and supernatural. Barclay was schooled in Descartes's rationalism and Calvin's predestinarianism, both of which were fraught with dualistic tendencies. For twentieth century Friends, of course, the frame of reference is markedly different. Scientific understanding has caused us to become critical of dualistic thought and forced us to try to integrate such philosophical and theological dichotomies. This affects how we relate the transcendence and immanence of God in creation and history.

If a tension is not maintained between the polarities of transcendence and immanence, the two merge and cease to complement each other. On the other hand, if too much emphasis is placed on transcendence, we end up with the deism of the eighteenth century, which taught that God created the world but thereafter had no significant interaction with it. This view was anathema to Friends. At the opposite extreme is the ever-popular pantheistic view, which so emphasizes the immanence of God in creation that God becomes everything and everything becomes God. Or, Gnosticism, which spiritualizes reality so that there is no place for the physical and material. Humanistic worldviews, especially in the twentieth century, culminate in a similar kind of monistic (as opposed to dualistic) thinking. In our own time, process theology has attempted to address the difficulties associated with these problems. To bridge the gap between the transcendent and immanent without losing the creative tension between the two is not easy. Process thought has tried to integrate the two realms and at the same time remain true to contemporary scientific constructs of reality and relativity theory in physics.

This debate poses a problem when Quaker mysticism leans toward Gnosticism to the point of becoming pantheistic and ends up adopting a humanistic perspective in psychology and human values. The result can be that "God," in any significant theistic sense, no longer prevails. Then Friends replace the two-story universe of the seventeenth century with a one-story or one-dimensional worldview, which means that basic distinctions between the holy and profane, the sacred and the secular—even between good and evil—are ignored, if not erased. Taken to its logical conclusion, this denies the presence of evil in the world, or sees it simply as the absence of the good. When this happens, Quakers are ridiculed for their false optimism. Historically, however, this was not the way Friends understood reality.

'That of God in Every One'

So what does this discussion of transcendence and immanence have to do with the Quaker understanding of God? The answer is that for liberal Quakerism it has resulted in such an altered view from early Quaker thought that one has to ask whether we are talking about the same God—namely, the God of the biblical and Christian faith out of which the Society of Friends came.

In this regard the key term that needs to be examined is "that of God in everyone." This phrase and its counterparts, used today by many Friends, go back to George Fox, the founder of the Quaker movement. Fox used the phrase a hundred times or more, but twentieth century Friends frequently have taken it out of context, altering some of its original meaning. Usually Fox used it to refer to "answering that of God" in another. For example, Fox admonished Friends to "be patterns, be examples . . . that your carriage and life may preach among all sorts of people, and to them. Then you will come to walk cheerfully over the world, answering that of God in everyone."[8]

Current usage of this phrase has a direct bearing on what Friends mean by "God."[9] In the first place, Fox's expression does not seem to appear in Quaker history between the time he used it and the beginning of the twentieth century when it was popularized by Rufus Jones.

Second, there has been a continuing debate about the meaning Fox intended. H. G. Wood once said, "It helps us little to say we believe in that of God in every man, if we do not know what we mean by 'that' and what we mean by 'God'."[10] Howard Brinton suggested that the phrase would be clarified by using Fox's own words when he referred to the "Light of Christ in every man," thereby personalizing God.[11] Others, including Henry Cadbury, have perhaps facetiously suggested that Friends declare a moratorium on the use of "that of God in every one," while Hugh Doncaster, in his 1963 Swarthmore Lecture at London Yearly Meeting, granted that the phrase has become "a Quaker cliche, hackneyed by much unthinking use …[yet] it is a good phrase and deserves refilling with a rich content, especially as it is likely to remain current among us."[12]

Various Quaker scholars believe that meanings attached to "that of God in everyone" have included: answering to a religious thirst or hunger reported in Fox's pastoral and ministry writings (Lewis Benson);[13] a human capacity within to respond to God's leading and bidding (Daniel Bassuk);[14] an objective ethical standard that is normative for decision-making (James Childress).[15] Whatever Fox's original intent, for many Friends "that of God in everyone" has become a doctrine of human nature, with only incidental reference to its God content. It is cited to affirm the worth and dignity of human beings and is used as a rationale for peace and justice issues. In these instances the phrase has been disengaged from historic Quaker experience and given a rational (or doctrinal) meaning that modern Friends want it to have. An example of this is stated by Glenn Bartoo: "Quakers believe there is 'that of God in every man,' equivalent in humanistic terms to 'the enlightened conscience,' or, more simply, that provided certain conditions are met, people choose the good."[16]

Insofar as "that of God in everyone" has theological meaning today, its association with Christ has been largely abandoned, whereas for George Fox this identification was essential. It has also come to mean that God, as they understand the deity, has been parceled out among all persons so that everyone has "a piece of God" within, and it is this that gives worth and dignity to human beings. This suggests a humanistic view of life devoid of a sense of God transcending creation, history, and humanity, which can easily revert to a form of pantheism antithetical to Fox's original sense of the greatness and goodness of God and the supreme presence and transforming power of God at work in the world. Thus, the net effect is a denigration of God and an exaltation of humanity. Somehow this belies Fox's overwhelming sense that "the power of the Lord is over all."

It is not without significance that Rufus Jones's last scholarly work on Quakerism, undertaken during his final illness in 1948, involved his counting the number of times Fox used "that of God in everyone" or its derivative in his *Epistles*. Jones counted fifty-one times.[17] It was out of his reflection on this that he penned these words, which were to have been included in an address to New England Yearly Meeting:

It is a nice question whether George Fox thought of this "more" [meaning "that of God in everyone"] as an inherent part of man's being as man, as the mystics of the fourteenth century under the influence of Plotinus almost certainly thought of the Divine spark in the soul, or whether George Fox thought of this "more," as Barclay certainly did, as a super-added bestowal of the Divine spirit; it is a question not easy to answer because he never clarified his position. But it is more probable that he agreed with the position of Barclay.[18]

The Evangelical Quaker View

We cannot leave our discussion of God without reference to the important stream of faith and practice broadly referred to as "evangelical Quakerism," which in the nineteenth century was often called "Gurneyite Quakerism" because of its association with the life, thought, and ministry of Joseph John Gurney, the eminent British Friend. This evangelical influence came largely from Anglican and Methodist sources prevalent in England, while at the same time Wesleyanism was increasing its influence on Friends in America. The Great Separations of Friends in America in 1827-28 reflected the extent to which this evangelical branch of the Society adhered to orthodox Christian belief.

Today the evangelical branch continues to reflect much of the Puritan thought that influenced early Friends, including a strong emphasis on Scripture as the primary source of religious authority. For this reason its doctrine of God, as compared with the liberal tradition, sounds much more orthodox and biblical. These evangelicals have never denigrated God by exalting human beings. Rather, because of too much Calvinistic and Wesleyan emphasis, they have often failed to do justice to the insights of Fox, Barclay, and others who took issue with many of the doctrinal points found in the Westminster Confession of Faith.

The culmination of evangelical (Gurneyite) thought among American Friends in the nineteenth century was the formulation of the Richmond Declaration of Faith at a general conference of Orthodox Friends in Richmond, Indiana, in 1887. This statement of faith was authored largely by J. Bevan Braithwaite, an influential evangelical Friend from England. Such a comprehensive doctrinal statement, covering a wide range of faith and practice, was unprecedented in the history of Friends. It begins with the following affirmation:

We believe in one holy (Isa. vi. 3, lvii. 15) almighty, (Gen. xvii. 1) all-wise, (Rom. xi. 33, xvi. 27) and everlasting, (Ps. xc. 1, 2) God, the Father, (Matt. xi. 25-27) the Creator (Gen. i. 1) and Preserver (Job vii. 20) of all things; and in Jesus Christ, His only Son, our Lord, by whom all things were made, (John i. 3) and by whom all things consist; (Col. i. 17) and in one Holy Spirit, proceeding from the Father and the Son, (John xv. 26, xvi. 7) the Reprover (John xvi. 8) of the world, the Witness for Christ, (John xv. 26) and the Teacher, (John xiv. 26) Guide, (John xiv. 13) and Sanctifier (II Thes. ii. 13) of the people of God; and that these three are one in the eternal Godhead; (Matt. xxviii. 19, John x. 30, xvii 21) to whom be honor, praise, and thanksgiving, now and forever, Amen.[19]

This statement of faith, Trinitarian and supported by scriptural references, became normative for evangelical Friends by the end of the nineteenth century. Since then the Richmond Declaration of Faith has been carried in most of the yearly meeting disciplines (commonly called Faith and Practice) of the Five Years Meeting of Friends (now called Friends United Meeting), and the yearly meetings of the Evangelical Friends International.

Another document that evangelical Friends claim as evidence of their orthodox view of God is George Fox's controversial "letter to the governor of Barbados" (1671).[20] The content of this letter coincides with the main points of the Apostles' Creed with respect to Trinitarian doctrine, except for the absence of the third article of the creed on the Holy Spirit. Although some have questioned the authenticity of the authorship of this letter because it seems out of character with Fox's general pattern of speaking and writing, it clearly shows a commitment to an orthodox Christian doctrine of God.

Because evangelical Friends today make up more than half of the

Quakers in North America, it is important to place their understanding of Christian and Quaker belief alongside the liberal interpretation given earlier. The liberal Friends (mainly in the Hicksite tradition—now called Friends General Conference) claim to remain true to early Quaker belief and practice, but a continuing debate has ensued between them and evangelicals about which Friends are most faithful to Fox's views in the seventeenth century. The fact is that both have departed from early Friends in language and in content of belief. For quite different reasons both groups have compromised what might be called the normative and authoritative nature of early Quaker faith and practice. Strangely enough it is the Wilburite Conservative Friends who have most consistently championed the "ancient testimonies and doctrines of Friends" as authoritative for Quaker faith and practice today. Both liberal and evangelical Friends have tended to pick and choose what suits them from early Friends and have adapted it to their particular branch of Quakerism.

The liberal justification for this is adherence to the traditional Quaker belief in continuing revelation, while the evangelicals defend their position by questioning whether Friends have been faithful to the biblical revelation. Thus the debate continues, with little foreseeable resolution that would present a united Quaker point of view about God or about other matters of belief in general.

Questions for Discussion

1. What has been the chief difficulty with the doctrine of the Trinity for Friends?
2. To what extent or in what way are Friends unitarian? Trinitarian?

(continued)

---

3. What is meant by the transcendence vs. immanence of God, and of what importance is this to Quaker faith?
4. Does "that of God in every one" express the essence of Quakerism? If so, explain what it means.
5. How do evangelical Friends differ from liberal Friends in their understanding of God?
6. What do Friends mean by "continuing revelation"?

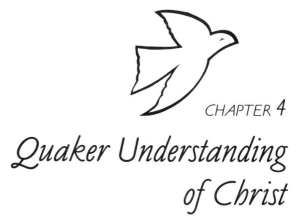

CHAPTER 4

Quaker Understanding of Christ

Anyone acquainted with the founding of the Quaker movement is familiar with George Fox's remarkable encounter with "Christ Jesus," an inward religious experience that changed the whole course of his life:

> But as I had forsaken all the priests, so I left the separate preachers also, and those called the most experienced people; for I saw there was none among them all that could speak to my condition. And when all my hopes in them and in all men were gone, so that I had nothing outwardly to help me, nor could tell what to do, then, Oh then, I heard a voice which said, 'There is one, even Christ Jesus, that can speak to thy condition,' and when I heard it my heart did leap for joy....And this I knew experimentally.[1]

One cannot read this confession and its ringing affirmation without concluding that Jesus Christ was crucial for Fox, although it is difficult to discern exactly what he meant by "Christ" and how this related to the Jesus of Nazareth.

Since the time of Fox, Friends have held differing views of Jesus and Christ, resulting from their lack of clarity about the relationship of the Christ of faith to the Jesus of history, not from any lack of belief in Jesus Christ. That uncertainty and lack of agreement continues to this day, although the over-riding tradition has been to emphasize the Christ Within at the expense of the historical Jesus. Moreover, as we have already discussed in other connections, Friends have never been precise about the meaning of the Christ Within and have often used the Spirit of God, Holy Spirit, Light Within, Christ Within, and similar terms interchangeably. Their chief concern has been to emphasize the importance of obedience to this inward spiritual guide rather than an emphasis upon following in the steps of Jesus of Nazareth. Some have even claimed to adhere to an inward "spiritual principle" without feeling the need to name it or relate it specifically to Jesus Christ.

Much of the difficulty and confusion surrounding Friends' understanding of Jesus Christ as a central focus of Quaker faith stems from their ambivalence about the importance of historical events as a means of revelation. Baron Von Hugel once accused Friends of being "historically ungrateful," by which he meant that they over-spiritualized religion to the point where they often failed to understand the important role of historical and cultural events in disclosing God's will in human affairs. Such over-spiritualization has often degenerated into gnostic devaluation of the physical and material in favor of the spiritual.

Review of Orthodox Christology

For all practical purposes George Fox and early Friends accepted the central doctrines of the church as recorded in the Apostles' Creed, even though some of the emphases they gave differed from the Puritan theology of their day. Rachel Hadley King points out that "although

George Fox believed that he had been taught not by man but by direct divine revelation, he nevertheless possessed a large amount of the Christian tradition by inheritance."[2]

A similar claim could be made for Robert Barclay, the first Quaker apologist to expound their basic beliefs. Since Barclay did not deal with every article of faith in his *Apology for the True Christian Divinity*, it seems apparent that he covered only those that Friends interpreted differently. This would indicate that on other counts he, like Fox, accepted much of orthodox Puritan belief.

Certainly Quakers since Fox and Barclay have had very divergent opinions about Christian orthodoxy. Although many factors played into the various separations of Friends in the nineteenth century, there were honest differences over theology, especially their views of the person and work of Christ. In this century Friends differ even more over these matters, and if we are to have a clearer understanding of these nuances we need to first review some of the main aspects of Christology in the Christian tradition.

When referring to the central figure of the Christian faith, it is important to refer to both "Jesus" and "Christ." Jesus represents the human side while Christ represents the divine — that is, the Messiah who was anointed and sent by God. In A.D. 451 the Council of Chalcedon declared that Jesus Christ was truly human and truly divine. So even though we use the terms separately, theologically they belong together. What this ultimately adds up to is the Christian doctrine of the Incarnation: "the Word became flesh and dwelt among us" (John 1:14), or to use Paul's assertion, "that God was in Christ" (2 Cor. 5:17-19).

God was revealed in Jesus Christ, and by means of this revelation we come to understand the nature and will of God. Jesus Christ is the bridge between God and humanity, between the spiritual world and the physical, material, cultural world of nature and history.

Reference was made earlier to the doctrine of the Trinity, which Friends took issue with on the grounds that it was extra-biblical and would violate the unity of the Godhead. For Christian theology, however, the Trinity preserves and sets forth the salient aspects of the Godhead. God the Father/Mother is the first person of the Trinity and is the source of life from which all creation flows. Jesus Christ, the second person of the Trinity, is the incarnation of God in history; it is here that the divine and human are brought together. Christians, including Quakers, have held that this divine Person (the eternal Christ) pre-existed the historical Jesus as the *Logos*, referred to in the opening verses of John's gospel. The third person of the Trinity is the Holy Spirit, who is the resurrected Christ promised to us as Counselor, Advocate, or Paraclete (John 14:15-17). This is clearly the Christ Within, which Quakers claim to be the living reality of God acting in and through us as individuals and through the world around us. Thus the Holy Spirit is God in action in the world here and now.

So far we have been looking at the person of Christ, also referred to as the nature of Christ.[3] We now turn to the work of Christ, and it is here that we take up the Atonement, or at least the various theories about the efficacy of Christ's death on the cross. It is interesting to note that the church never spoke in unison on the Atonement as it did on the Trinity and other aspects of the person of Christ as reflected in the church councils of Nicea (A.D. 325), Constantinople (A.D. 381), and Chalcedon (A.D. 451).

The assumption behind the Atonement is that humanity is in a condition of sin or separation from God. Some attribute this condition to the Fall, while others claim that responsibility for this separation rests squarely with us as human beings. In either case sin is a condition from which we cannot extricate ourselves apart from the prevenient grace and action of God on our behalf.

Essentially there are four theories of Atonement: 1. The ransom theory of Origen maintained that Christ's death was a ransom paid to the Devil to break the power of evil and free persons from the power of sin. 2. Anselm's satisfaction theory held that because of the depth and seriousness of human sin only God, through the death of the Son, could render satisfaction and restore the honor of God. 3. A slight modification of this theory, made during the Protestant Reformation, was the penal or substitutionary theory which stated that Christ bore the punishment due humanity. 4. Finally, there was Abelard's theory, sometimes called the moral influence view. Whereas Anselm held to an objective atonement in which the mind and heart of God was changed toward sinful humanity, Abelard advanced a subjective theory proposing that the change had to take place in the mind and heart of the sinner. Thus, as one contemplated the death of Christ on the cross, one was moved to repentance through the vicarious suffering of Christ.

It is easy for Friends to become impatient with this kind of Christological enquiry. At the same time we need to remind ourselves that historically Christology has been regarded as a scandal and an affront to the rational mind. And if sin and guilt are to be removed through grace and forgiveness, then making ourselves vulnerable before God and the community of faith is essential.

Because we believe that the miraculous power of God was at work in the birth, life, and death of Jesus Christ, it is only reasonable to assume that the final mystery was enacted by God in the resurrection of the crucified Christ. Whereas God through Christ seemed defeated by the forces of evil at the cross on Good Friday, Christ's victory over sin and evil was accomplished by breaking the power of the demonic forces of Satan. Faith says that the Resurrection was not an illusion or hallucination, but that Jesus Christ was indeed raised to newness of life through the power of God.

In considering the legacy of Jesus Christ one must also remember his role as rabbi and teacher of the new law as reflected in the Sermon on the Mount; his three years of performing the mighty works of God in a healing ministry; his parables which formed part of his public ministry; and his proclamation of the coming of the kingdom of God. In terms of the messianic mission of Jesus it has long been customary to speak of the three offices of Christ: prophet, priest, and king. Mainstream Christianity has stressed primarily the priestly and kingly roles, while the radical and sectarian churches have emphasized Christ's prophetic role.

With this all-too-brief summary as background, we shall now turn to the Quaker response to these interpretations of Christology, indicating the particular emphases Friends have given to the significance of Jesus Christ.

The Quaker Interpretation of Christ[4]

Since it is impossible to discern a single, consistent pattern of Christological thought among Friends, either historically or today, primary attention here will be given to their early understanding of Christ and its relationship to the central principle of Quakerism— namely, the Light of Christ Within. In his treatise on early Quaker Christology, Maurice Creasey indicates that their understanding of Christ was couched in the language of Scripture and their aim was to try to recover "primitive Christianity" as the norm. The results of their efforts are not systematic and often appear conflicting. However, Creasey is able to draw some important conclusions from his study.

The clear impression left upon the mind after a prolonged study of their [early Friends] writings is that of the profound sense which Quakers had of the supreme and all-embracing significance of Christ as the Power and Wisdom of God in creation, revelation and redemption. So great was their emphasis upon this singleness and wholeness and unity that they tended to minimize anything that seemed to imply distinction, or discontinuity. In every age and in relation to every man, Christ, they felt, had exercised these same functions: the only difference lay in the mode of their exercise, whether in Christ's pre-incarnate, incarnate or risen and glorified state.[5]

At the beginning of his study Creasey makes the important observation that the central doctrine of early Quakerism was "the inner light." But he adds that

… it is less generally recognized that the features of this doctrine which are truly distinctive of Quakerism are those which result from the Quaker attempt to express, in terms of this doctrine, a profound interpretation of the person and work of Christ. It is thus a Christological rather than an anthropological doctrine.[6]

One of the clearest early Quaker witnesses to the identification of Christ with the Light was from a tract by George Bishop in 1665:

By the word Light, and the Light within, we mean Christ the light …. Now this is not Natural Reason … but when we speak of the Light and this Light within, we only intend Christ; the light of Christ; Christ the light; the true light that lighteth every man that cometh into the World; which Reason is not …. Of this we speak; and we mean nothing else when we speak of the Light, and this Light within.[7]

A similar affirmation comes from Robert Barclay: "Yea, they believe this Light, Grace and Seed to be no other, but a measure of that Life and Spirit that was in Christ Jesus."[8]

Such statements are repeated over and over, says Creasey, thus confirming this view as normative for early Friends. And in another place he writes:

> … for early Friends all that they said about the Light they intended to be understood as being said about Christ; and second, that when they spoke of Christ they meant a Christ whose activity in relation to the world of men comprehended all that which in the New Testament and in the mainstream of Christian doctrine was normally distributed among the Logos or Word or Son, the historic Jesus Christ, the risen and glorified Christ, and the Holy Spirit.[9]

While Friends openly opposed Trinitarian doctrine, in their own personal religious experience they believed in the three persons of the Trinity: Father, Son, and Holy Ghost. This is evidenced by George Fox's assertion that "the Father of life drew me to his son by his spirit."[10] Creasey reports that Friends also objected to the word "person" as applied to the Trinity because it was too abstract and carnal and did not honor the Divine Being.[11] They preferred to speak in experiential language about the way in which God is manifested in the Father, Son, and Holy Ghost.

The Pre-Incarnate Christ

Creasey provided a framework for the early Quaker understanding of Christ by establishing three categories: the pre-incarnate Christ, the incarnate Christ, and the risen and exalted Christ. Friends greatly emphasized the revelatory significance of the pre-incarnate Christ, in keeping with the Pauline and Johannine traditions of the New Testament. They believed this pre-incarnate eternal Christ to be God's agent of creation and redemption as set forth in Colossians 1:15-20:

> He is the image of the invisible God, the firstborn of all creation; for in him all things were created, in heaven and on earth, visible and invisible, whether thrones or dominions or principalities or authorities—all things were created through him and for him. He is before all things, and in him all things hold together. He is the head of the body, the church; he is the beginning, the first-born from the dead, that in everything he might be pre-eminent. For in him all the fulness of God was pleased to dwell, and through him to reconcile to himself all things, whether on earth or in heaven, making peace by the blood of his cross.

Reflecting on early Friends' dependence on this Scripture, Creasey declares:

> …that Christ as the Light, prior to the incarnation, was the "power of God unto Salvation," by whose secret and inward working in all ages … God was seeking to lead men into the state for which, in creation, God intended them.[12]

George Keith, a seventeenth–century Friend, spoke of the "pre-existent humanity of Christ."[13] At the same time, Friends claimed that this "pre-existent Christ" had a "saving activity" that left no one without access to God. Indeed Friends clearly stated that one did not have to know the name of Jesus to benefit from the saving grace of God. This was part of the universal saving doctrine of early Friends.[14] Robert Barclay made it clear, however, that Christ's death and suffering were necessary in order for human sin to be remitted, and that anyone to whom Christ had been revealed was duty bound to acknowledge the efficacy of the Atonement.[15]

The Incarnate Christ

George Fox was more concerned with the moral and spiritual benefits of Christ than with the divine-human nature of Christ, unlike mainline Christendom. And though Friends subscribed to the Johannine affirmation that "the Word became flesh" (John 1:14), they were primarily interested in the spiritual continuity that the Incarnation effected between the divine and the human.[16] Fox claimed that separateness between God and humans applied only to the unreconciled and unredeemed.

Friends were sometimes accused of the fourth century Appolinarian heresy which held that the body and soul of Jesus Christ were human while the rational spirit—the center of Jesus' person—was replaced by the divine *Logos*.[17] This may have been reflected in Isaac Penington's assertion that the person of Christ was divine, whereas Christ's humanity was a garment that clothed his divinity.[18] Creasey points out, however, that Barclay denied this Appolinarian accusation by claiming that Christ was mediator by virtue of "having been with God from all eternity, being God himself, and also in time partaking of man ... ."[19] Barclay spoke of Christ "in whom the fullness of the Godhead dwelt bodily . . . [who was] the Eternal Word, which was with God, and was God, [who] dwelt in that holy man [Christ]."[20]

Fox and other early Friends held that the incarnate Christ inaugurated the new covenant dispensation, thus doing away with the need for the Hebrew ordinances and ceremonies. As Fox so often said, "Christ had come to teach his people himself;" therefore the ritual and ceremony of the old covenant had been superseded by the spirit of God expressed through the living Christ within.

One question that seems never to have been clearly resolved for seventeenth century Friends was whether the historical redemptive work of Christ was a necessity. The problem was how to relate this to the "pre-incarnated saving activity in the heavenly humanity of Christ" referred to earlier. Rachel Hadley King suggests that Fox's emphasis upon the Light of Christ Within would seem to eliminate the need for the Christian revelation and, therefore, Christ's redemptive role. Perhaps somewhat surprisingly she says:

> Fox's central position can be held without reference to historical Christianity. His theory that the universal saving light within is the only teacher and authority is too general to be specifically Christian. There is no logical need for the incarnation and the passion in Fox's central conceptions. When Fox talks about Christ's dying for us and redeeming us, he is simply using inherited terminology without coordinating it with his other thought. . . . There is an inescapable externality about the incident of Jesus' death at Jerusalem, which Fox cannot fit with logical ease into his general belief in the inwardness of all that is necessary for salvation.[21]

King concludes, however, that ". . . in spite of his [Fox's] attempt to rely wholly upon immediate experience, he held that his [Christ's] personal revelation was fully consistent with the revelation that had come to men in the past."[22]

Fox believed that Christ offered himself on the cross as the supreme sacrifice, the "Lamb slain from the Foundation of the world." Yet Fox did not put much emphasis on the outward cross. Rather, "the cross of Christ was the power of God within that is in opposition to, or goes contrary to the evil in human nature."[23] This is another example of Fox's emphasis on the inwardness of religion rather than the outward forms and events of history. This relationship between the inward and outward sometimes seems tenuous, although Fox undoubtedly believed, either from experience or out of tradition, in the outward Christian revelatory events of history.

The Risen Glorified Christ

In the theological climate of the seventeenth century it was difficult for anyone to accept the idea of a living Christ in any meaningful way. John Bunyan found it incomprehensible that Christ, who must have been "four or five feet long," could possibly live "in" a believer![24]

Friends claimed to know this resurrected Christ by various names: the Christ Within, the Light Within, and the Holy Spirit (John 14:25-26); but they did not insist that one had to know this Spirit within by the name of Jesus or Christ. Clearly, however, it was not to be confused with conscience or with reason. Neither was it to be confused with Scripture. But because it was identified with the same Spirit or Light that pre-existed the historical Jesus, it was understood to be the universal witness available to all persons who responded in obedience to God. Creasey refers to Barclay's claim that only as Christ comes to be formed in a person through personal holy obedience can God's saving grace become efficacious. But this Light can also be denied one. Early Friends spoke of "the day of visitation" that comes to everyone, but may also be taken away or passed by so that it is no longer available.

Justification and Sanctification

One of the marks that distinguished Friends from their Protestant Reformation contemporaries was their refusal to talk about justification by faith apart from sanctification. Nor did they believe in two works of grace—justification and subsequent sanctification—as became true in the Wesleyan tradition. Friends held that one was not justified before God until one was sanctified—that is, made holy. But they were quick to point out that this was not salvation by good works. Rather, justification and sanctification were two complementary aspects of the work of Christ.[25]

Fox claimed that the aim was to bring one into the state of Adam before the Fall. In such a state one was freed from guilt and the power of sin. This led naturally to a doctrine of Christian perfection, which became a basic principle in the witness of Fox and early Friends. (Because of the importance of the doctrine of perfection in Quaker history we shall deal with it more thoroughly in the next chapter, "Quaker View of Human Nature.") Quakers were sometimes charged with Pelagianism because of their belief that they could extricate themselves from sin. But it is important to note that early Friends attributed the possibility of perfection and sanctification to "the working of the indwelling Christ," not to human effort, and they did not believe that one could be freed from temptation to sin.[26]

Offices of Christ

As Lewis Benson points out, the threefold office of Christ—prophet, priest, and king—had been a part of church tradition for centuries. It is through these offices that the redemptive work of Christ is carried on. Benson asserts, however, that Calvin was responsible for making this into dogmatic theology.[27] Benson goes on to say that although Calvin introduced the prophetic role of Christ into theology, his main preoccupation was with "Jesus' messiahship . . . determined by his priestly and kingly offices." By so depicting Jesus, "he was conforming to the main tradition in the church from the second century onward."[28]

The offices or functions of Christ were also a central teaching of George Fox, but he went beyond the traditional threefold designation. In his study of early Quaker Christology, Creasey points out that "Fox regularly extends the titles of the offices in a manner which reflects unmistakably his profound sense of the supreme and manifold significance of Christ."[29] He then proceeds to spell out the way in which Christ, according to Fox, exercises his offices:

> Christ is Counsellor: "Do you hear His Voice from Heaven, concerning your Heavenly state?" He is a Shepherd: "Do you follow him? Do you know his Voice?" He is Priest: "Do you feel his Blood sprinkling your Hearts, and his pure Water washing you?" He is Prophet: "Do you hear him in all things? Doth he reveal the Father to you? Doth he open the Book of Conscience to you? Christ is King: "Doth he rule in your hearts by Faith?"[30]

Fox's position on the offices of Christ was radical because it applied not just to individuals but was to be exercised corporately on behalf of the church. "It is this radical emphasis on the headship of Christ over his Church that forms the foundation of the Quaker conception of Worship, Sacraments, and Ministry," asserts Creasey.[31]

However, Lewis Benson and the New Foundation Fellowship maintain that George Fox was not just another reformer, in the tradition of Luther and Calvin. Fox, they say, was a revolutionary calling for a return to the apostolic ministry of the New Testament church. Benson writes:

> The great new fact of Fox's revolutionary Christianity is that Christ is alive and present in the midst of his people in all his offices, including the office of prophet. Fox asserted that the recovery of the gospel that had been lost from the apostolic times would lead to the recovery of the righteousness and the Christ-governed community that had been lost "since the apostle's days."[32]

Fox's complaint was that the Christian churches were interested in a Savior who would forgive sin but not in a Christ with moral power to overcome sin. In other words, the churches focused primarily on the priestly office of Christ. According to Lewis Benson:

> In the gospel that Fox preached the prophetic office of Christ plays a part in his saviourhood which is not subordinate to his priestly and kingly offices. The general proclamation, "Christ has come to teach his people himself," contains a message about Christ the prophet like Moses, who is to be heard and obeyed in all things. *This* is the gospel that had been "lost" since the apostles' days and which was now being preached *again*.[33]

Benson contends that although Fox preached a revolutionary gospel, the second and third generations of Quakers separated the prophetic role of Christ from their message about the Light Within, thus losing its moral power as well as its revolutionary character. He asserts that after Fox's death the message that "Christ has come to teach his people himself" ceased to be proclaimed, and as a result:

Fox's whole functional Christology went into eclipse. From the beginning of the eighteenth century onward we hear nothing more about Christ the prophet. The Quakers began to think of their whole faith and practice as having one center and one starting point—the doctrine of the "Inner Light."[34]

To summarize this survey of early Quaker Christology, Creasey draws three conclusions he believes to be significant:

1. Early Friends attempted to bring within the compass of the person and work of Christ the whole range of divine dealings in creation and redemption.

2. Early Friends attempted to interpret all moral and spiritual experiences of non-Christians, pre-Christians, and Christians in terms of the judging and saving activity of God in Christ.

3. Early Friends attempted to derive all church doctrine pertaining to worship, ministry, and sacraments from the offices Christ exercised in the midst of his people. [35]

Twentieth-Century Quaker Views of Christ

Before concluding this discussion of Quaker Christology, we need to look at several interpretations of Christ that have held sway in the twentieth century or that have competed with other major claims. These can be generally divided into Quaker liberalism and evangelical Quakerism.

Evangelical Quaker View

Competing with and predating Quaker liberalism is an evangelical Quaker perspective on Christology and other matters of faith and practice. The roots of this movement go back to the latter part of the eighteenth and the early nineteenth centuries when Quakerism was impacted by the influence of Wesleyan Methodism and the Church of England. This was particularly true of Friends in England and the Quaker ministers who found their way to America, including Joseph John Gurney.

These Friends placed less emphasis on the Light Within and more on the Holy Spirit and scriptural authority. Instead of espousing the Light of Christ Within, they focused on the historic Christ who died on Calvary. Thus, the work of Christ was stressed in terms of Christ's substitutionary death on the cross for the sins of humanity.

In the nineteenth century evangelical Friends were represented by the Gurney Orthodox tradition. They believed that they were faithful to the heritage of Friends going back to Fox, Barclay, and Penn; but they also adopted some of the characteristics of evangelical Protestantism in faith and practice (especially in forms of worship and ministry), which made their fellow Quakers of liberal persuasions very uncomfortable.

Liberal Quaker View

The earliest Quaker liberalism is best represented by the views of Rufus M. Jones (1863-1948), who came out of the Orthodox tradition of New England Friends but was known most of his life as a Quaker mystic in the liberal tradition. Contrary to the beliefs of some of his critics, Jones was clearly Christ-centered in his views of Christian and Quaker faith. The following quotation bears witness to this while at the same time reflecting his stance on Christology.

Christ for the (Christian) mystic is the Eternal Lover, the Bridegroom of souls. He is the crown and culmination of divine revelation, and in His life and person He has forever made visible and vocal in our world the mind, the will, the heart, the character of God. He is an eternal manifestation of God, striking his being into bounds at a definite period of history, being born in human form in time and space, living a life of limitless love and forgiveness and going the way of the cross in unspeakable agony of suffering that He might forever show the consummate way of the spiritual life, and finally triumphing over defeat and death in a resurrection which proves Him to be a new type and order of spiritual life. He is thus the head of a new race, the first of a new series, the founder of a new Kingdom, the revealer of a new way of living. His divine love wooing, pleading, appealing, enduring all things, suffering with those who sin, and sharing the common tragedies of life with us, is the power unto salvation for all who understand and see its significance. To be saved, then, would be to live by the impact and inspiration of His life, to feel the appeal of His personality, the contagion of His spirit, the drawing force of His unspeakable love, the operation of His invisible and eternal presence within, making the old life impossible and recreating in the inner man a new will, a new heart, a new mind and a new natured self, so that the old self with its instinctive tendencies no longer lives, but Christ at the center as the force and spring of action, makes all things new.[36]

Jones's viewpoint here was representative of a large segment of liberal Quakerism well into the twentieth century, but in recent decades the mood has divided in two directions. The major trend has been to examine Quakerism from a universalist/world religion and social action perspective, and the second has been a reaction to the mystical reinterpretation given George Fox and early Friends by Rufus Jones. This latter movement was spearheaded by Lewis Benson (1906-1986) just before World War II and has gained significant momentum in the years since.

In recent years it has become embodied in the New Foundation Fellowship where its objective has been to re-examine early Quakerism, particularly Fox's life and writings, and to make this normative today.

Several references have already been made to Lewis Benson's interpretation of Christology as he attempted to reflect upon Fox's message. Those who have pursued this point of view no longer regard themselves in the liberal camp of Quakerism; instead, they see themselves as a "neoorthodox" movement within the Society of Friends engaged in recovering the early Quaker vision and preaching message. This has had a significant impact on liberal Quakerism and beyond, but numerically these neo-orthodox have been outnumbered by those who join mystical inwardness with social action and by those who wish to stress Quaker universalism.

Quaker Universalism

As a result of the shift in liberal Quaker thought, one of the most lively issues today is whether Quakerism is a universal religion and, if so, in what sense. Is it universal within the context of Christian faith, or is it universal in the sense that it no longer takes for granted its historic identification with Christianity?

Although the Society of Friends has always claimed that the Light of Christ Within is universally available to all humanity through the incarnate *Logos*, never until this generation of Quakers has it been suggested that Friends disengage themselves from their Christian roots in order to speak to the conditions of persons of all faiths and cultures. This fact poses an entirely new understanding of Quakerism and calls for an explanation of how Friends should deal with this situation.[37]

Early Quaker literature clearly reveals that Fox's followers accepted the biblical and Christian pathway to God and salvation. At the same time, built into this was a universalism based on the affirmation that all persons are endowed with the Divine Light (John 1:9); and because the Light was identified with Christ, this opened the way for a universalist interpretation of the doctrine. Barclay expressed it this way:

> God, who out of his infinite love sent his Son, the Lord Jesus Christ, into the world, who tasted death for every man, hath given to every man, whether Jew or Gentile, Turk or Scythian, Indian or Barbarian, of whatsoever nation, country, or place, a certain day or time of visitation; during which day or time it is possible for them to be saved … ; Secondly, that for this end God hath communicated and given unto every man a measure of the light of his Son, a measure of grace, or a measure of the Spirit . . .; Thirdly, that God, in and by the Light and Seed, invites, calls, exhorts, and strives with every man, in order to save him; which as it is received and not resisted, works the salvation of all, even of those who are ignorant of the death and sufferings of Christ.[38]

Further, Barclay says that "all men, even the heathen, may be saved: for Christ was given as a 'light to enlighten the Gentiles,' Isaiah 49:6," even though one may never have heard of the name of Jesus Christ.[39] But Barclay explains that "salvation lieth not in the literal, but in the experimental knowledge," so that it is the experience of the saving Light that counts.

Many Quakers today who want to identify with their heritage do so by retaining the Light but no longer relating it to Christ. In fact, they now prefer to speak of "that of God in everyone" as the universal principle of Quakerism in place of the Light of Christ Within. In response to this, the late Francis Hall wrote an article, "Christian Quakerism and Universal Quakerism," where he makes this conclusion:

Does this end the matter? Must it be concluded that such Friends are not truly Quaker? I believe not, because there are modern-day barriers to believing that Jesus is the Christ that are as powerful as was the barrier of lack of knowledge which prevailed at the time of Barclay.[40]

The barriers Hall is talking about include: (1) the immoral persecution and warfare perpetrated in Christian history; (2) the hypocrisy of church members; (3) the conflict between Christian faith, as often articulated, and modern science; and (4) the introduction to the Western world of knowledge about other religions and cultures. From this Hall concludes "that the universal, saving Light can be working salvation among these modern people who know the history [of Christianity] but do not accept it because of one or more of these barriers."[41]

Another point of view is expressed by John McCandless in his pamphlet, *Quaker Understanding of Christ*, where he takes issue with those who regard "Christian truth" and "universal truth" as polarities or points of tension. He says: "If we do not believe that Christian truth is universal truth, or if we do not believe that universal truth is Christian truth, then we ought not to be Christians. A Christian is a person who believes Christian truth is universal."[42] McCandless counters Quaker universalism further by saying that "when it is asserted that some Friends are 'not Christ-centered, but are God-centered, or Spirit-centered, or Light-centered,' the question immediately arises: in what light, what spirit, what 'god' are they centered?"[43] He suspects that it is the same universal light that informs the rest of society, and he suggests that it may be a form of social and intellectual elitism to which universalist Friends feel drawn.

At the other end of the Quaker spectrum are many Friends, especially in the evangelical tradition, who would share the views of the late

Everett Cattell expressed at the 1970 St. Louis Faith and Life Conference of Friends: "No one has a right to use the word Quaker to describe a system which is not Christocentric."[44] This view is more fully spelled out by Arthur Roberts, an articulate spokesman for the Evangelical Friends position today.[45]

So the debate goes on and shows no signs of being resolved. Yet the Society of Friends has moved into a new day, and its survival may well depend upon a rediscovery of its identity within the context of its own history, coupled with an effort to interpret that identity in a relevant way to a constantly changing world.

Questions for Discussion

1. In what way do Friends over-spiritualize outward historical events such as the life of Jesus?
2. Does the Quaker emphasis on the Light of Christ Within eliminate the need for Christ's atonement on the cross?
3. What is meant by the Christian doctrine of Incarnation, and does it have relevance for Friends?
4. How did early Friends understand the relationship of justification and sanctification in the salvation process?
5. What is meant by the offices of Christ (prophet, priest, and king), and where have Friends placed the emphasis?
6. How would you describe Quaker universalism? Is there more than one Quaker view of this?

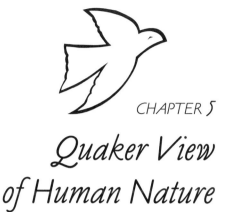

CHAPTER 5

Quaker View of Human Nature

S ince the dawn of human consciousness human beings have been inquisitive and curious about themselves. A modern parable of this insatiable desire to understand ourselves is expressed in the story of an insane person who was found rushing about the house frantically looking in all of the cupboards and closets and crawling under beds, obviously searching for something. When asked what he was looking for, the person responded: "I am trying to find myself."

Part of what it means to find oneself is to know oneself and eventually to understand oneself, and this calls for the ability to discern the meaning of human nature. Human nature in turn is defined in terms of understanding the essential characteristics of what it means to be human.

This is a crucial question, of course, when dealing with doctrine and theology and a definition of faith, for it involves an understanding of human nature as it relates to the problems of sin and evil and how to overcome them.

absence

Humanity in the Creation and the Fall

In the beginning God created the heavens and the earth…. Then
God said, "let us make man [and woman] in our image, after our
likeness …." And God saw everything that he had made, and
behold, it was very good (Gen. 1:1, 26, 31).

Historically and to this present day Friends would agree with this
biblical account of creation, thus standing in the biblical tradition that
subscribes to the fundamental assumption that creation is good, including both male and female human beings. Dealing with this on a personal
level is more difficult, however, for our own experience tells us that not
all is good. We are always conscious of the presence of evil in our
world—evil being the opposite of good. There is probably no rational
understanding of evil that will completely satisfy us, but we still have to
take it into account.

What would Margaret say?

In the book of Genesis evil is accounted for by the fall of humanity
from the original state of goodness and perfection in creation. And
whether or not we accept the biblical story as true in fact, human beings
find it true to reality. A widely accepted contemporary view is that the
Fall was not an historical event but is something everyone experiences
in his or her own personal history. Whatever happened "back then,"
there is a clear sense that "something went wrong" so that now part of
what it means to be human is to know the difference between good and
evil and at the same time feel responsible for choosing the good over the
evil.

Creation in the Image of God

From the Hebrew-Christian perspective the most sacred thing we can say about human beings is that they are created in the image of God *(imago Dei.)*.[1] Genesis 1:26 asserts that man and woman were created in the "image" and "likeness" of God, interpreted as a state of unity and righteousness in the creation. Because of the Fall this condition has been lost, or at least impaired.

The early church Father, Irenaeus, claimed that in the Fall, human likeness to God was lost, while the image (namely, our rational and moral capacity) was retained. This came to be the standard Catholic view, later held by Thomas Aquinas. But during the Protestant Reformation, Luther and Calvin claimed that in the Fall, not only was the human likeness to God lost, but also that only a relic of the *imago Dei* was left. While human rationality and the sense of right and wrong remained as part of the image, it was damaged so that human reason and the sense of moral accountability became flawed and therefore were not always trustworthy.

Because human beings lost their original state of unity and righteousness, they are now in a state of separation or alienation from God. Thus the eternal quest of man and woman is to try to recover their original relationship with God so that their wills are united with God's will. This is the eternal quest for salvation: to be made whole again and to be at one with the Creator.

The *imago Dei* is very much akin to the early Quaker idea of the Seed, the Light, or "that of God in everyone." All of these terms express the God-given potential or capacity to respond to God's grace and transforming love. It is important to note that all of these capacities were understood by early Friends to be *from* Christ and that this Christ is identified with the *Logos* set forth in the theologies of Paul and John in the New Testament. Thus Friends are in the mainstream of biblical and Christian thought with respect to the *imago Dei* presuppositions of religious faith. In fact, Friends have believed more than most other

Christians that this God-given capacity (i.e., grace) can enable human beings to overcome sin and to become what they are intended to become.

Friends Understanding of Sin

In dealing with the problem of human sin we need first to set it in the larger context of the problem of evil. Traditionally philosophers and theologians have thought of evil as the large category that stands opposite good; within this "not good" category they then make a distinction between natural evil and moral evil, or sin.

Natural evil includes all the natural causes of pain, suffering, and death, such as floods, tornadoes, hurricanes, earthquakes, and diseases affecting life on earth. These are events or conditions over which we have little, if any, control; and since we are not morally responsible for them, the law recognizes them as "acts of God." *we are responsible*

The other large area of the "not good" is that for which we are responsible and accountable, namely, moral evil. In the Christian and biblical tradition we call this "sin" because as responsible human beings we are accountable to God for our conduct. Sin, therefore, is personal rather than abstract; it involves defiance of God's will resulting in acts of disobedience. *are we children !?*

There is a common notion that Friends do not believe in sin and evil, or at least the charge is that they do not take them very seriously. This is true in part, but it is also a distorted understanding if looked at in historical perspective. It is true that Friends never preoccupied themselves with theories of human depravity in the same way that their seventeenth century Puritan counterparts did. Also, it is true that a faith that stresses the inwardness of religion, that emphasizes the image of God in humans, that places a premium on the Light Within can lead to a sense of self-sufficiency in moral actions and away from any sense of need for moral and spiritual redemption, including the need for a savior. But in spite of certain innovations in Quaker thought during recent generations, there is no question that early Friends took sin and evil seriously.

Of his own conversion experience, George Fox declared: "For all are concluded under sin, and shut up in unbelief as I had been." [2] Fox believed that through the disobedience of Adam and Eve all persons lost their "original righteousness." Both Adam and Eve fell "from the purity, holiness, innocency, pure and good estate, in which God placed them. So Adam died, and Eve died; and all died—in Adam."[3] Sin, therefore, is universal. While it is rooted in Adam's and Eve's disobedience, sin continues and multiplies because of our disobedience.

In Douglas Gwyn's study of the early Quaker view of sin and evil he describes Fox's view of sin as "going out from the Truth."[4] It is through disobedience that we become alienated from God and separated from the truth. Gwyn points out that for early Friends evil did not really exist; rather, "evil is [being] out of the Truth." In the Fall, human beings turn away from "inward unity with God" and turn to the idolatry of false gods. This idolatry then becomes the condition of human sin. Rather than being the source of evil and sin, Adam and Eve become types or examples of this kind of idolatrous behavior. For Fox this interpretation of sin was both personal and corporate in the life of the church.

Other early Friends had equally strong views about the chronic nature of sin. Isaac Penington believed that humanity was by nature in "a state of sin and darkness; a state of death and misery; a state of enmity against God; a state accursed from God; exposed to his wrath and most righteous judgments, both here and hereafter."[5] Keeping in mind the "relic of the *imago Dei*," which Luther and Calvin believed was retained after the Fall, it is perhaps surprising that as a Quaker Penington should write:

Men speak of the relics of the image which the first man had: Ah!

poor deceived hearts! What relics of the life are there in a dead man? What relics of purity in a man wholly degenerated and corrupted? Nay, nay; the spiritual image, the divine image, the eternal life, the pure power and virtue is wholly lost; and there is nothing left.[6]

In spite of humanity's lost condition the hope in Penington's view is to be found in his doctrine of the Seed. He declared that "the earth [i.e., sinful human nature] is not so much as prepared to receive the seed, until the Lord sends his plough in the heart."[7] It is not entirely clear whether this is a principle of redemption resident in human nature, but it is clear that divine action is needed to activate the Seed.

Robert Barclay was no less certain of the sinful propensities of human nature. When questioned about this, he said:

All Adam's posterity, or mankind, both Jews and Gentiles, as to the first Adam, or earthly man, is fallen, degenerate, and dead ... that not only their words and deeds, but all their imaginations, are evil perpetually in the sight of God.[8]

Fox, Penington, and Barclay concurred that sin is humanity's deliberate disobedience of God's will. However, they differed about sin as an inherited condition. For Fox and Penington, sin was an act of disobedience as well as a condition of human nature. Because of Barclay's great concern not to condemn infants to damnation, he refused to ascribe Adam's guilt to anyone until that person had adopted Adam's sin through an act of disobedience. Thus infants who were not yet accountable had not transgressed God's will until they consciously committed sin.[9]

During the middle period of Quakerism two nineteenth century

Friends were representative of the views on the subject of sin: Joseph John Gurney represented the evangelical Orthodox position, and Elias Hicks represented the liberal (Hicksite) point of view.

It is no surprise to find Gurney espousing a reasonably orthodox Christian position. He said that through "the transgression of our first parents . . . man is a fallen creature, by nature the child of wrath, prone to iniquity, and absolutely incapable of true holiness and happiness, unless he be born again of the Spirit." Gurney also believed that the atonement of Christ was necessary to overcome sin and gain salvation. Thus he asserted that "it is only through the precious blood of Jesus Christ, shed for us on the cross, that our 'iniquity is forgiven,' and our 'sin covered.'"[10] Lest one conclude that he had departed from his Quaker heritage, it is important to couple these statements with his affirmation about the freedom of the will made possible by the Light acclaimed in the Gospel of John.

> Every human being has this *freedom of will,* with a sufficiency of light and power to direct its operations; but this powerful light is not inherent in any man's nature, but is graciously *bestowed by him who is the true light, that lighteth every man that cometh into the world.*[11]

Elias Hicks seems less clear in his statements about human sin. Nevertheless he did affirm sin as part of the human condition when he said:

> But from this happy state [i.e., before the Fall] man fell, by a wrong use and abuse of those powers and capacities conferred on him as a free agent, and without which he neither could have known or (sic) served his God: therefore, man's fall was altogether

an act of his own choice, contrary to known duty; and had it not been so, he could not possibly have felt guilt and condemnation for what he had done.[12]   *Shame*

In a number of places Hicks spoke of the fallen nature of persons. From this he concluded that human sin originated in self-will, which he seems to equate with the fallen nature. At the same time human beings are responsible for their own sin, in which case sin is not inherited. Whether an act is good or evil seems for Hicks to depend on the intention behind the act rather than the result of the act, as reflected in the following statement:

> For although a man in his fallen state may do a moral act, that in itself is a right work, yet, doing it for his own pleasure and will, and not because it is agreeable to the will and pleasure of his Creator, it cannot be accepted as a good act, because the motive and principle were evil, being selfish and not of God.[13]

On the subject of the Cross and the Atonement Hicks's view was similar to Fox's. Hicks internalized and spiritualized the cross, but he was not clear about the importance of the outward cross for post-biblical times.

> Now I consider that the offering of the body of Jesus Christ on the outward cross, applied only, as a matter of redemption, to the Israelites, redeeming them from the curse of that covenant . . . by the outward death of their Messiah. And this outward redemption of the soul from sin by *the life*, or *spiritual blood of Christ*, inwardly sprinkling our consciences, and thereby enabling us to die to sin as he died for sin; by which we are redeemed from dead

works, to serve the living God in the newness of life, which make, and alone can make, the true Christian.[14]

Although Hicks differed from Gurney and Orthodox Friends in his view of the nature of sin and its cure, he did not ignore sin as integral to the human condition. He agreed with historic Quakerism about the need to be responsible for one's sin, and he recognized the need for an inward transformation as the basis for overcoming sin. He differed, however, regarding the role of the historic Christ in human redemption. At that point he internalized and spiritualized the cross as the means by which redemption took place.

Changing Attitudes Toward Sin

At this point a word about Quaker history is important. The eighteenth century was marked by Quietism, which in mood and thought retained most of the theological assumptions of early Friends but in practice turned inward, while at the same time distrusting reason. Because of its inward bent it automatically de-emphasized the outward. Against this background during the late eighteenth and nineteenth centuries evangelicalism had an impact upon Quaker faith and practice. This meant movement toward more orthodox interpretations of religious authority, including heavier reliance on the Scriptures, more traditional Protestant views regarding Christology, and a gradual acceptance of more traditional patterns of worship and ministry.

By the end of the nineteenth century, however, another change took place in the Society of Friends. From mid-century onward a new Christian liberalism began to influence the society, so that by the beginning of the twentieth century Quaker liberal theology was in the ascendancy. Liberal leadership came to the fore to replace the eighteenth century evangelical leadership. These trends prevailed on both sides of the Atlantic, resulting in the virtual disappearance of Quaker Quietism. Quaker evangelicalism pretty much vanished in England but persisted with growing influence in America, as well as in some of the Quaker mission areas of the world, especially in East Africa and Latin America. Quaker liberalism, on the other hand, became widely acclaimed by Friends, with strongholds in both England and America. Paralleling these developments was a comparable change in Quaker understanding and evaluation of human nature and the problems of sin and evil.

This new trend in Quakerism is best illustrated by the views of Rufus Jones, whose life and influence spanned the first half of the twentieth century.[15] At the turn of the century Jones and a group of liberal Quaker scholars tried to redefine and restate Quaker faith and practice in light of the impact of modern science, especially the influence of Darwinism. They did the same with the new historical-critical method of biblical studies. Their objective was to speak relevantly and persuasively to the youth of the day who were beginning to question some of the basic assumptions of traditional orthodox belief.

Jones has probably had more influence on Quaker thought and practice in the twentieth century than any other single person. With respect to sin he differed markedly from his Quaker forebears, for he held that sin originated not from some abstract concept of Satan and the Fall but from our human struggle to emerge from the biological processes of nature. At some point in our emergence "instinct" and "moral insight" collide and conscience is born. Thus human beings come into a knowledge of good and evil. At this conscious level we no longer need to be governed by the unreflective push of instinct. Instead, we enter a stage of struggle between the lower impulses and the higher ideals and aspirations striving to guide and shape our lives. Sin results when our human will (or self) surrenders to the impulses and drives of our "lower natures" as opposed to the values and ideals of our "higher natures."

Jones believed there is a cumulative effect of sin in terms of its consequences. Sinful acts produce a "set of the nature," and the only way to overcome this is to undo the habit of sinning and develop in its place a pattern of good behavior. However, Jones did not regard human nature as fundamentally bad or depraved. He believed that if we exercise our rational nature to master our lower impulses, then we are on our way to mental and spiritual health. If we learn to love goodness and become attracted to it, we will naturally choose the good rather than evil.

> To apologize for sin as though it belonged to man's nature, to assume that he is a worm in the dust and necessarily evil are contrary to the entire idea of the Quaker. Fallen he may be, a stubborn sinner and degraded being, but that is because he is not what he was meant to be.[16]

The roots of Jones's view of sin and evil go back to the influence of Platonic philosophy, where sin arises out of conflict between the spiritual and physical realms. In the Hebrew-Christian tradition sin has always been highly personal—an act of disobedience to God's will. In the Platonic tradition sin is seldom regarded as a personal affront to God or a defiance of God's will; instead, evil is the absence of the good, and sin is equated with error or misjudgment. If the passions of the lower self disturb the rational calculations of the higher self, then error in judgment is bound to follow. Jones believed this view of sin also corresponded with Saint Paul's view expressed in Romans 7:9-25, where the apostle speaks of "a lower nature [which] dominates us and spoils our life."[17]

Douglas Steere, who follows in the same spiritual heritage, seems to diverge somewhat from Jones's view. This can be seen in the following observation he made regarding sin as dealt with in Saint Augustine's *Confessions*.

> In the light of this I begin to see what is meant by this hereditary defiance of God called "original sin," which is so prominent in the treatises of Augustine. I begin to see that he is only writing a commentary upon Jesus' holding up as the object of his most bitter invective not the sins of the body but the sins of pride, of selfishness, of hardness of heart, of self-righteousness. And in this emphasis of Jesus and Augustine there seems to be a major cleavage with Greek thought as expressed in such a mind as Plato. For Plato there is no talk of sin of the mind such as pride, that may keep man from blessedness. For Plato, mind does not block or blind itself. It is matter that keeps the mind in darkness. It is the unruly steeds of the body and its lustful appetites that are opposed to the character of the mind. It is the biological that retards the psychological, and if the mind could dominate all, if by proper education the psychological could assume supremacy over the biological, for Plato all would be well.[18]

Although Steere is impressed with Augustine's analysis, he warns against his doctrine of sin that, apart from his *Confessions*, "remains a pre-Christian legalistic formula, a forbidding and vicious dogma."

Elton Trueblood, another twentieth-century Quaker, was less optimistic about human nature and referred to the "chronic" and "indigenous" nature of human sin.

> The point is that man is, *qua* man, a sinner, even in his virtue. He may be able to overcome or to hold in check the sins of the flesh,

but his temptations will not end thereby. In fact all agree that the sins of the spirit are far more terrible than are the sins of the flesh . . . . Of all the sins that of spiritual pride is probably the worst and the most damaging. It is thus that Paradise is lost.[20]

Trueblood injects a caution, however, for those who would overemphasize the "indigenous" character of sin. "A philosophy which would cut the nerve of moral effort is an evil philosophy and this is what is evil in either sheer optimism or sheer pessimism."[21] Moreover, he points out that the doctrine of human sin never describes the "whole truth" about human beings. It is the Gospel that teaches "that God reaches out to every man and this we need to know far more vividly."[22]

In the face of two world wars and the present tragedies of our day, much of the optimism about human nature that prevailed earlier has been superseded by a more realistic view. In addition to the quotations drawn from Steere and Trueblood, other Quaker documentation of this could be given. At the same time, a large segment of American Friends who identify themselves as evangelicals have always retained a strong doctrine of sin. Arthur Roberts, writing from that perspective, states: "Friends recognize that man is depraved, in that he cannot of his own power or inclination find salvation. Quakers are not so much optimistic about man as they are optimistic about the power of Christ to save man."[23]

The Social Nature of Sin

Another dimension of sin that has become a major concern in the twentieth century is its social and institutional nature and consequences. The Social Gospel movement that arose out of nineteenth century ideas popularized the belief that humankind is caught up in a network of social evil, much of which has been inherited. This concept of social sin was dramatized early in this century by Walter Rauschenbusch and at mid-century by Reinhold Niebuhr. Their impact upon social thought has not gone unnoticed by Friends, although they have been slow to understand the real meaning and relevance of such views. Cecil Hinshaw observed that although early Quakers did not subscribe to a utopian view of the world, he doubts whether they understood as well as we do today "the extent to which man in his corporate relationship in society normally engages in evil that far transcends personal sin." He states further:

> Our vision of a new world and culture must never blind us to the hard fact that even good men are caught up in the magnetism of corporate sin and held by a power of attraction difficult even for psychologists to explain.[24]

The crux of the problem for Friends is that they seldom make any distinction between a personal ethic and a social ethic. In both its evangelical and liberal manifestations Quakerism is highly individual-istic. It espouses a personal ethic that is supposed to be applied not only to the affairs of the individual but to all the corporate decisions of society. The Third World Conference of Friends held at Oxford, England, in 1952 declared: "We call upon people everywhere to … behave as men and brothers, to substitute the institutions of peace for the institutions of war."[25] One could cite many Quaker statements in this vein.

Friends seem to have difficulty comprehending the complexity of group behavior or understanding why organizational and national affairs cannot be conducted on the same personal basis as the affairs of the family or the small community. Kenneth Boulding quite rightly points out that "only small organizations can be personal." In the same reference he says that "a good deal of harm has been done by interpreting the moral ideal of the 'brotherhood of man' . . . to mean that all human organization must be like a family, in its looseness of organization and its complexity of personal interaction."[26]

Douglas Steere, on the other hand, took issue with what he called the "collectivist theologians" of the 1930s and 1940s who attempted to give a theological rationale for what they believed to be a valid and relevant contemporary social ethic.[27] Although he recognizes the service they performed in their study and analysis of corporate sin, his general criticism of this point of view sounds much like George Fox's warning when he criticized the Calvinists of his time for "preaching up sin."[28]

These references serve to illustrate the fact that although Quakers are noted for their social concern and their attempt to demonstrate a living faith that produces a vital social ethic, their approach continues to be strongly personal. They place such a premium on the individual that even in their own groups they manifest a lack of understanding of the corporate complexities and ambiguities inherent in social organization. Groups of people involve a multiplicity of claims to be considered for every choice made, and clear-cut decisions are rare. Because Friends, too, have to live with these situations all the time, they are often obsessed with guilt feelings about the fact that decisions are sometimes ambiguous.

When we take seriously the social as well as the individual nature of sin, it soon becomes clear that we as human beings are "radically historical" creatures. All of our past choices inevitably condition our present choices. Thus, we are victims of our own sin. As early Quakers knew so well, our only hope for release from this bondage is that the cycle of sin and evil will be broken by the transforming "power of the Lord." It is to this hope that we now turn.

Perfection: Quaker Search for Integrity

The popular notion that Quakers have an optimistic belief that sin and evil can be overcome is not without substance. Friends have always held the deep conviction that "things do not have to be the way they are." They have always believed that by the "power of the Lord" (or by the grace of God) we can experience victory over sin, evil, and death. These beliefs and hopes form the basis for the Christian doctrine of perfection held by George Fox and the early Friends. A similar doctrine was promulgated by John Wesley and the Methodist movement a century later; and in the nineteenth century the search for Christian perfection continued under the influence of the Methodist revivalists and subsequently became embodied in the holiness movement of evangelical Friends. When liberal Quakerism of the early twentieth century partially eclipsed the evangelical upsurge of the nineteenth century, religious idealism became the watchword for those who believed that the kingdom of God could be realized here and now.

Reflecting the perfectionistic bent of early Friends, Cecil Hinshaw and Elfrida Vipont Foulds, from quite different perspectives (one American and the other British), have claimed that the essence of Fox's message was expressed in his demand for *integrity*. Other terms used by Friends to give voice to the perfectionistic motif would include Thomas Kelly's call for "holy obedience"; R. W. Tucker's emphasis on "revolutionary faithfulness"; and Dean Freiday's substitution of the word "maturity" for "perfection" in his modern English edition of Barclay's *Apology*. The Christian search for salvation expresses something of the same objective, namely, our common need to be recalled into a state of reconciliation with God, which entails the integration of our wills with God's will, thus fulfilling our search for spiritual integrity. In the fourth century Augustine expressed the same longing when he uttered his famous prayer: "Thou hast created us for Thyself, and our hearts are restless until they find their rest in Thee."

Thus a central characteristic of early Friends was their belief that a life of Christian perfection and holiness was possible. They believed that whereas all died through the disobedience of Adam, all shall be made alive through the obedience of the Perfect One—Christ. Of Fox's own conversion experience he said:

Now I was come up in Spirit through the flaming sword into the paradise of God. All things were new, and all the creation gave another smell unto me than before, beyond what words can utter. I knew nothing but pureness, and innocency, and righteousness, being renewed up into the image of God, and Christ Jesus, so that I saw I was come up to the state of Adam which he was in before he fell.[29]

Fox did not hold that human beings would never sin again, but that as they remained obedient to the Light of Christ they would continue in the life of perfection. Although Isaac Penington did not write extensively about the doctrine of Christian perfection, he nevertheless agreed with Fox when he said, "Is it not the will of Christ that his disciples should be perfect, as their heavenly Father is perfect? . . . Will God dwell in an unholy temple? Will he dwell where sin dwells?"[30]

Barclay devoted an entire Proposition to the subject of perfection, and the following excerpt presents the main theme of his argument:

We do believe, that to those in whom Christ comes to be formed, and the new man brought forth, and born of the incorruptible seed, as that birth, and man in union therewith, naturally doth the will of God, it is possible so far to keep to it, as not to be found daily transgressors of the law of God.[31]

Even though he believed in the possibility of Christian perfection, Barclay also made it clear that the life of perfection does "admit of growth." We are not expected to reach the holiness and perfection of God "but only a perfection proportionable and answerable to man's measure . . . [which] enables [us] to answer what he [i.e., God] requires of us." There is also the possibility that those who "do not diligently attend to that of God in the heart" will lose this state of perfection. "And we doubt not," said Barclay, "but many good and holy men, who have arrived to everlasting life, have had divers ebbings and flowings of this kind." On the other hand, he declared, "I will not affirm that a state is not attainable in this life, in which to do righteousness may be so natural to the regenerate soul, that in the stability of that condition he cannot sin."[32] Barclay added a personal note to confess that he never arrived at such a state of perfection himself, yet he defended the possibility that it could happen.

Salvation

In most books on systematic theology this discussion of the *imago Dei* potential in every human being as well as our human proneness to sin and disobedience would be placed in the context of the Christian doctrine of salvation. Thus it is appropriate to say that if *sin* means separation and alienation from God through disobedience, then *salvation* means the reuniting of our human wills with God's will in order to experience reconciliation with our Creator.

Paul Tillich pointed out that the root meaning of salvation can be traced to the Latin *salvus* (or *salus*), meaning "health" or "wholeness."[33]

Thus "to be saved" can mean "to be made whole again" or "to be restored" to a condition of spiritual health.

Most traditional discussions of salvation also speak of the Christian understanding of *redemption* as a process involving stages of spiritual development. Beginning with the assumption that human beings are in a state of sin and separation from God, the first step is to reverse this by *repentance* and *conversion*, which means to change (turn around) one's direction of life. This entails a human response based on an act of free will. Next comes *justification*, or God's acceptance and affirmation of us. Justification is seen as a necessary action on the part of God to complete the process of salvation, the assumption being that we cannot save ourselves, but by the grace of God we can be restored to a right relationship with God.

A number of Christian groups, including the Friends, believe that the redemption/salvation process is not authentic until we enter into holy obedience to God. In some traditions, including evangelical Quakerism, this stage of spiritual development is called sanctification—that is, being made holy in the presence of God. Arrival at this point enables one to say with Kierkegaard, "I will to do one thing only and that is to do the will of God." For Friends such an understanding of the redemptive process corresponds with what Fox meant by Christian perfection; sanctification, holiness, and perfection are in effect synonymous terms. However, there is an important difference between Friends and other Christian groups at this point, for Friends do not make a distinction between justification and sanctification in the redemptive process. They believe that one is not fully justified before God until one is sanctified—that is, brought into holy obedience and spiritual unity with God.

Likewise, Friends have taken issue with Wesley's first and second work of grace to effect justification and sanctification following conversion. (Quakers speak of "convincement" rather than "conversion." For them "convincement" represents "the initial step on the long road to Christian perfection.")[34] They believe there is one work of grace—namely, that if one lives "in the virtue of that life and power of God" (to quote George Fox), then one can come into a "perfectly" restored relationship with God.[35] Such a state of sanctification led Fox and early Friends to believe that they could live as if the kingdom of God was already present, and not some future event.

Finally, Friends have never been of one mind about whether the Light of Christ Within is sufficient for salvation or whether the atoning death of Jesus Christ on the cross was necessary to make reconciliation with God possible. (Note references to this earlier in this chapter, as well as in chapters 2 and 4.) The evangelical tradition of Friends has held that the atoning work of Christ on the cross is essential to salvation. Liberal Friends, on the other hand, have emphasized the Light of Christ Within (or, more recently "that of God in every one") as the basis for spiritual reconciliation with God. Another way of expressing this difference is that liberal Friends emphasize Christian nurture in place of Christian redemption, whereas evangelical Friends emphasize Christian redemption *and then* Christian nurture as the basis for growth toward the life of Christian perfection.

In keeping with the Puritan tradition of their times, early Friends took it for granted that the sacrificial death of Christ was essential and that the efficacy of the Light Within depended upon it. Fox said in his *Journal*: "For I saw that Christ died for all men, and was propitiation for all, and had enlightened all men and women with his divine and saving light and that none could be true believers but who believed in it."[36] Likewise Robert Barclay understood that the redemptive and saving Light of Christ presupposed his atoning death: "This light is no less universal than the seed of sin, being purchased by his death who tasted death for everyone: 'For as in Adam all die, so in Christ all will be made to live.' (I Cor. 15:22)."[37] It is significant to note that in the early nineteenth century Joseph John Gurney seems to have happily joined both views when he said: "Between the declaration of Paul, that Christ gave himself 'a ransom for all,' and that of John, that 'he lighteth every man that cometh into the world,' there is surely a most satisfactory and delightful accordance."[38]

Concurrent with Gurney's view, Hicksite Friends in the nineteenth century placed primary emphasis on the inward redemptive work of Christ as the essential and all-sufficient Quaker principle, creating a spiritualization of the redemptive process by disengaging the Light Within from its identification with the historical Christ. In some cases this was carried so far that the Light was regarded as a natural endowment without any need for a transcendent referent. The net result has been a tendency toward a humanistic understanding of the self, which is quite alien to traditional Quaker reliance upon "the power of the Lord" to overcome sin. Thus, whether there is need for Christ's atonement has been an issue for Friends through the centuries and continues to be so today.

In conclusion we may say that Friends have always held a high view of human nature grounded in the creative and redemptive power of God. Although they have generally recognized the sin of human beings, both as an act of free will and as a condition of the self, their chief preoccupation has not been with sin but with the availability of the power and grace of God to recreate the human situation in all its dimensions, personal as well as social. Moreover, Friends hold that if we are faithful to God we will be enabled to overcome sin and death. Such a spiritual victory, it is believed, will take the form of a life of holy obedience to God here and now and will carry with it an eternal hope for humanity in the total economy of God's purposes.

Questions for Discussion

1. What is the condition of human beings in creation with which the Bible and Christians (including Friends) are in agreement?
2. Compare the "image of God" concept in Genesis to the early Quaker view of the Seed, Light, and "that of God in every one."
3. Distinguish between the biblical concept of sin and the general (philosophical) concept of evil.
4. How did Rufus Jones's view of the source of sin differ from his Quaker forebears?
5. To what extent do Quakers recognize the corporate nature of sin as compared with individual responsibility for sin?
6. Describe the early Quaker concept of Christian perfection. How would it compare with Thomas Kelly's "holy obedience" or Howard Brinton's "living up to the measure of the Light given us"?

CHAPTER 6

Quaker Understanding of the Church

B ecause Friends place so much emphasis on the dignity and worth of the individual, as well as on the Light Within and firsthand religious experience, it is sometimes thought that they have no corporate understanding of their religious faith as it relates to the church. This misconception overlooks their long-standing reliance upon corporate fellowship manifested in the Quaker meeting, which is essential to a full knowledge of how Friends function spiritually and how they conduct themselves in group life.

Historically Friends have tended to be anti-church and pro-sectarian, and because of the traditional distrust of the institutional church and organized religion, they have not been recognized as having any fully developed doctrine of the church. Insofar as they have such a doctrine, it is clearly "low church" in character and tradition rather than liturgical, although some would argue that Quakerism actually constitutes a third form of Christianity (alongside Protestantism and Roman Catholicism).

In the seventeenth century Robert Barclay regarded Friends as holding to a distinctive form of Christianity. In the twentieth century students of Quakerism as diverse as Howard Brinton and Lewis Benson have made a similar distinction.[1] Looking at it in terms of worship forms, Brinton points out that Roman Catholic worship centers on the altar or the celebration of the Eucharist; Protestant worship focuses on the sermon or the preaching of the Word from the pulpit; and Quaker worship centers on the immediate presence of God experienced within the heart.[2]

Even though historically Friends emerged out of the radical movements surrounding seventeenth century English Puritanism (and thus Protestantism), it can be persuasively argued that at the very beginning the Society of Friends was marked by certain unique characteristics that set it apart from the main Christian traditions of the time. Friends believed they were recovering the true New Testament church or, in the words of William Penn, "primitive Christianity revived." George Fox claimed that the church had been apostate and in the wilderness since the time of Constantine, if not earlier, and he regarded it as his mission to reclaim the true church of Jesus Christ.

Quakers also have certain affinities with the radical reformation of the Anabaptist and free church traditions. Friends find much in common with many of these groups in the areas of church polity and discipline and in their passion for ethical purity patterned after the Sermon on the Mount. This has been most fully expressed through the Quaker Peace Testimony which Friends share with the Mennonites and Church of the Brethren in modern times. Although all of these groups would like to consider their standards of faith and practice as normative for all Christians, the fact is that the mainline churches regard their radical witness as sectarian. This would suggest that they clearly do not belong in the "church" typology of Ernst Troeltsch, and as a consequence they are usually classified as sectarian.[3] (Troeltsch set forth church, sect, and mysticism as three types of Christianity.) In more recent times, however, as John Timothy Terrell shows, Friends have departed from their earlier so-called sectarian patterns of church life, and a large segment of them have moved toward traditional patterns of denominationalism in church organization and practice. This, he believes, has been reflected in the past century through the development of pastoral and programmed forms of worship and ministry.[4]

Friends have always understood the church to be the fellowship of believers, so in this sense it is quite possible to discern a Quaker understanding of the church stemming from the beginnings of the Society. Also, they spoke of their places of worship as "meetinghouses" and referred to the gathered body of worshipers as "the meeting." In this century, however, many in the pastoral/programmed tradition, who lean toward evangelical doctrine and practice, refer to their places of worship as "churches." Friends of a liberal and unprogrammed persuasion object to the use of the word "church" altogether, so much so that they have lost touch with its New Testament and early Quaker meaning and usage.

A Quaker Perspective

To gain a better understanding of the Quaker view of the church it will be helpful to summarize some of the main characteristics of the church from their perspective, beginning with their objections.[5]

1. Friends objected to making salvation the function of the clergy by the preaching of the Word and the administration of the sacraments, in place of the direct action of the Holy Spirit to spiritually transform lives.

2. They objected to restricting ministry and the priesthood to a particular class of people ordained to a particular office. They believed that potentially everyone can be a minister of Christ and receive a gift

in ministry.

3. They objected to the church's lack of concern for practical righteousness. They believed that living in the will of God was possible here and now by the transforming grace and power of God. Thus the Christian is called to live as if the kingdom were already here.

4. They objected to public taxation (payment of church tithes) for the support of the church. Rather, they believed in voluntary support and a free Gospel ministry.

On the positive side, Friends emphasized:

1. The church is a gathered holy community whose purpose it is to carry the Gospel into all the world. Because they believed that the church in this sense is God-ordained, they leaned toward a theocratic rather than democratic view of church and state. Thus final authority rests with God (*Theos*) rather than with the people (*demos*). Later Friends adopted a more democratic understanding of how God's will is discerned and obeyed by individual persons.

2. The church is a fellowship of people gathered by Christ and made alive by God's Spirit. The church is not, therefore, a building or an institution bound by the organizational structure of time and place.

3. The chief mark of the true church is righteousness and obedience to Christ. Christ, the head, orders the church in worship, ministry, mission, and service.

4. The principle of unity in the church is the Light of Christ and the Spirit of God. As all seek the Light they shall be brought into a common sense of unity.

In an important article, "Being a People of God," Charles Thomas spells out more carefully what he calls the "marks" of "the people of

God."[6] The term "people of God" reflects the biblical vision of a "covenant people" committed to serving God. This, Thomas believes, parallels the early Quaker understanding of the church, and he lists the following marks of such a people:

1. The people of God are a community with a vision of Truth (early Friends spelled Truth with a capital T).
2. The people of God are a community of people committed to the covenant of God.
3. The people of God have a living relationship to the Spirit of God.
4. The people of God are a prophetic people rather than a cultic people concerned with liturgical tradition.
5. The people of God are a people on mission.
6. The people of God are a worshiping and praying people.
7. The people of God are morally and ethically sensitive.

Father Donald Nesti, who has been involved in Catholic Quaker studies, wrote a doctoral dissertation on early Quakers, including a section on "Early Quaker Ecclesiology."[7] In it he pointed out that the Quakers were preoccupied with the apostate institutional church as the Antichrist and therefore rejected the visible, temporal church with its humanly contrived forms: the paid ministry, liturgy, relics, ritual, vestments, holy days, religious rites, and sacraments. Instead Friends called for a totally "spiritual ecclesiology."[8] They believed that the true church was gathered out of the world into the Spirit of God. Membership in this church was by faith in Jesus Christ and required conversion and regeneration. Christ was the spiritual head of this church, but one did not necessarily have to know the name of Christ in order to be joined with it.

Another point Nesti made, one that is important to our understanding of the early Quaker view, is that Friends were caught up with the apocalyptic and messianic expectations of their age. They believed that the "Day of the Lord" was at hand. As Fox declared, "Christ has come to teach his people himself," and now it was possible to live by the power of the resurrected Christ and become a part of the true church of Christ without form or structure. Nesti also spoke of the sacramental aspects of early Quaker ecclesiology, indicating that the outward signs of this ecclesiology consisted of the visible unity of the Christian fellowship, the sanctified life of holiness lived by its members, and the exercise of a spiritual ministry as a means of spreading the light, grace, and truth they proclaimed. It was a ministry rooted in Old Testament prophecy and New Testament *diakonia* (service). At the same time it was marked by the free gift of the Spirit and in this sense was charismatic.

Worship

Gladys Wilson, in her little book *Quaker Worship*, suggests that four elements are emphasized in Fox's concept of worship: silence, communion, ministry, and fellowship.[9] First was silence, for "centering down in the silence" was the unique manner in which Friends from the beginning entered into worship, although they more commonly used "waiting upon the Lord" rather than the word "worship." Second, communion with God and one another was believed to be both possible and essential in Quaker worship. Elton Trueblood once suggested that Friends should be able to go away from their meeting for worship and say "that they had been to holy communion today." Third, ministry was a central element of worship, sometimes seeming to take precedent over worship. And fourth, Friends clearly believed that fellowship, or the New Testament concept of *koinonia*, was not only central to worship but could be counted on as an important by-product of worship. This is the sense of being "members one of another," and it is the means by which differences fade into the background so that unity can prevail.

Although early Quakers avoided symbolism and art forms to depict reality, the well-known Quaker painting by Doyle Penrose, *The Presence in the Midst*, graphically presents the historic Quaker understanding of worship. Penrose painted the famous Jordans meetinghouse outside London with the figure of Christ set in the midst of Friends gathered in silent worship. It is often remarked that the concept of worship portrayed here bears a striking resemblance to the Catholic Mass (the Eucharist), with the real presence of Christ in the midst. Because Friends historically believed that, according to George Fox, "Christ has come to teach his people himself," Penrose's painting lucidly presents the "gathered meeting" around the feet of Christ without benefit of priest or ordained minister and without the need for liturgical ceremony. Such "silent waiting upon the Lord" in an attitude of expectancy represents both the attitude and posture characteristic of traditional Quaker worship.

The Scripture that best supports this form of worship is found in John 4:23-24: "But the hour is coming, and now is, when the true worshipers will worship the Father in spirit and truth, for such the Father seeks to worship him. God is spirit, and those who worship him must worship in spirit and truth." This frequently quoted passage was joined by Fox's admonition that Friends should "meet together in the Name of Jesus, whose Name is above every Name, and Gathering is above every Gathering."[10] In his *Epistles* Fox identifies "the Name of Jesus" with "the Light of Christ," sometimes using these terms simultaneously.[11] Wherever Fox refers to "waiting in the Light" he maintains that this Light proceeds from Jesus Christ.[12] So the prerequisite for early Quaker worship was to "meet in spirit and in truth" and to "meet in the Name of Jesus."

Fox and early Friends believed the scriptural admonition to worship "in the Spirit" was to be interpreted as silent waiting before God, and many beautiful passages in the writings of early Friends give testimony to their belief that Christ meant for them to worship in this manner. For example, Francis Howgill wrote:

The Lord of heaven and earth we found to be near at hand, and, as we waited upon Him in pure silence, our minds out of all things, His heavenly presence appeared in our assemblies, when there was no language, tongue nor speech from any creature. The Kingdom of heaven did gather us and catch us all, as in a net, and His heavenly power at one time drew many hundreds to land.[13]

In a similar vein Robert Barclay gave this testimony about the transforming power he experienced upon his first visit to a Friends meeting:

When I came into the silent assemblies of God's people, I felt a secret power among them, which touched my heart, and as I gave way unto it, I found the evil weakening in me, and the good raised up, and so I became thus knit and united unto them, hungering more and more after the increase of this power and life, whereby I might feel myself perfectly redeemed.[14]

Friends worship is not determined by holy days or liturgical acts of celebration or re-enactments of past events. Worship is a "now event" under the direction of the Holy Spirit. It is believed that the old covenant, which relied on ceremonial rites, ritual, and sacrifices, was replaced by the new covenant instituted by Christ, which called for the immediate and real presence of Christ in worship. This requires the worshiper to enter into a hearing and obeying relationship with Christ rather than conforming to ceremonial rites and creeds. Worship is not dependent upon the office of a minister or priest but is ordered by Christ within. God is the actor and the worshiper is the reactor or responder.

Although Friends worship has always called for centering down in silent "waiting upon the Lord," silence has never been an end in itself. Silence is a means to an end and thus becomes a form of worship, though clearly less structured than most forms. Such "silent waiting upon the Lord" does not have to occur in a sacred building or place. A worshiping group can become a "gathered meeting" wherever two or three come together and the Spirit of God is present.

During the Quietistic period silence prevailed and vocal ministry almost disappeared. This became the common practice for more than a hundred years, from the middle of the eighteenth century to the middle of the nineteenth century. Frequently meetings of one to two hours were held in complete silence. Not only did these Friends fear that in speaking to the gathered meeting they might "run ahead of their Guide" in ministry, but they also preferred mystical communion in the silence to meetings where prophetic ministry was heard. Although the Quietistic period exhibited genuine spirituality, it was also a time of "low and almost desolate" estate for many meetings.[15]

During the second half of the nineteenth century worship became modified in those meetings that adopted pastoral/programmed patterns of worship and ministry. For the most part these meetings still refused to use liturgies, formulated prayers, litanies, and creeds, and they also refrained from observing the sacraments (or ordinances). They did, however, add music, spoken prayers, Scripture reading, offerings, and prepared messages, while still believing the gathering was under the leadership of the Holy Spirit. In recent years there has been some experimentation in pastoral/programmed meetings to allow for more silence in worship and to invite the active participation of worshipers in vocal ministry and prayer.

Whether a Friends meeting experiences the life and power of the Spirit in its worship is not contingent on its being either programmed or unprogrammed. Meetings of both forms exhibit times of shallowness and times of great spiritual depth. In either case Friends need to be vigilant in nurturing the life of the Spirit in their own lives in order to enrich their periods of gathered worship. Forms of worship are important, and some seem preferable and more appropriate to Friends, but none can guarantee aliveness to the Spirit of Christ apart from the faithfulness of individual members.

Ministry

George Fox's early followers responded enthusiastically to his ministry, and ministry became one of the central elements of Friends worship from the beginning. The natural leaders of the Quaker movement were the ministers, for Friends had a great missionary impulse to carry the "everlasting Gospel" not only throughout England and to the Continent nearby, but to the far ends of the earth, especially colonial America.

An important characteristic of Quaker ministry in the early period, as well as throughout its history, was the "prophetic" element of ministry, which is called forth by God. It was patterned after the prophetic ministry of the prophets of Israel in the Old Testament. Such ministry was not about "prediction of things to come," but it was a calling by God to "proclaim the word of the Lord for the day." It was a Spirit-led ministry which caused those who spoke to quake in the power of the Spirit.

Friends ministered through various kinds of meetings, which were recognized as avenues for spreading the Gospel. In addition to the steady growth of what we might call the local meetings, called "settled meetings," Friends proclaimed the message to any who would hear it. Such outreach efforts were called "threshing meetings" where the unconvinced were challenged with the message. Also, almost immediately a need developed for the traveling ministry, such as the "valiant sixty" who went out from Swarthmoor Hall in northwest England to carry the Gospel message. In London Fox and his colleagues established the "morning meeting," which met every Second-Day (Monday) morning, to give guidance and direct ministers to where they should go during the coming week; at the same time it provided surveillance of both "the approved ministers" and, subsequently, "the approved writings" of Friends. This marked the beginning of disciplinary control over an otherwise free Gospel ministry.

With changing times and the demise of the first generation of leadership, substantial changes took place in the Society of Friends. Although their numbers increased after the Act of Toleration in 1689, most of these Friends were the children and grandchildren of the first generation. Almost invariably they were less committed and had less of a sense of calling, and the inspiration and life of the Society began to wane. The eighteenth century, especially after 1740, marked the beginning of the Quietistic period of withdrawal. As a kind of testimony against the Age of Reason, Friends were counseled to turn to the Inward Teacher and cautioned against "exceeding the measure" of the Spirit that guided them. This counsel was especially directed toward those who engaged in ministry. Also, in 1702 London Yearly Meeting issued "Cautions and Counsels to Ministers," which caused some to question their gift of ministry.[16] The cumulative effect of all this was a withdrawal from ministry into silence.

Lucia Beamish's important study, *Quaker Ministry: 1691-1834*, establishes four reasons for the major changes in the ministry in the mid-eighteenth to the mid-nineteenth century.[17]

1. With the crystallization of the offices of elders and overseers as distinct from the ministry, the power and authority of the elders and overseers grew in comparison to that of the ministers.

2. Quaker ministry spread to the new Pennsylvania colony in America where Quakerism was no longer persecuted but was the "established religion" of William Penn's "Holy Experiment" in government.

3. The tightening of discipline in the eighteenth century had a dampening influence. The fear of individual enthusiasm in ministry and disorder in worship called for stricter guidelines in the form of Advices and Queries, enforced by the elders and overseers. In 1755 London Yearly Meeting revised and enlarged its Queries, marking the beginning of a "reform" period in the Society. Outward uniformity of behavior sometimes became the content of ministry, replacing a ministry of spiritual awakening. Paradoxically, women in ministry increased markedly during this same period of time.

4. The swing to silence in meetings obviously impacted the traditional practice of vocal ministry. Because ministry had often become lifeless, Friends were counseled to sit in an attitude of inward prayer and silence. Thus the "life of the meeting" came to be measured by the quality of the silence and not by the quality of ministry.

Neave Brayshaw points out that even as Friends met corporately, they met "alone" with God. The result of this individual isolation in worship undermined the feeling of fellowship that had prevailed in seventeenth century Quaker worship. Friends lost their sense of "membership one with another" as they moved deeper and deeper into silent worship.[18]

There has been a continuing debate about why Friends moved toward Quietism during this period. Why did they have such a suspicion of "creaturely activity" based on their sense of the moral ruin of the individual? Rufus Jones and Elbert Russell claimed that Friends were overly influenced by the Quaker apologist, Robert Barclay, who took human sin seriously and stressed the incapacity of human nature apart from the regenerative action of God. Russell also notes the belief that Quakers were influenced by the continental Catholic Quietism of Molinos, Fénelon, and Madame Guyon, which was part of the Protestant and Catholic Counter-Reformation, especially in France.[19] Lucia Beamish, on the other hand, has a different analysis. She believes the impact of Methodism (the ministry of John Wesley and George Whitehead) on the Society of Friends caused them to withdraw into Quietism in a strong reaction against Methodist revivalism and emotionalism. She says that Quaker ministry was a response to a "call" of God and was often infused with dread and anguish rather than religious enthusiasm and evangelical emotionalism. Quietistic Friends believed that ministry was subject to "the Cross," which they interpreted as an inward spiritual burden to be borne in faithfulness to Christ.

Not until the second half of the nineteenth century did Friends in England and America awake from their quietistic manner of life. In England, as a result of an important study done by John Stephenson Rowntree entitled *Quakerism Past and Present*, (1859), Friends began to re-examine their style and practice of ministry and to examine their reasons for disowning so many members for "marrying out of meeting" or for other offenses cited by the Discipline. Very soon London Yearly Meeting began to relax its century-old restrictive standards; as a result a new openness developed and Quaker practices were updated to fit the times.

On the other side of the Atlantic the 1850s and 1860s marked the beginning of major changes in the worship and ministry of Orthodox (Gurney) Friends. Most were a result of evangelical Christian practices that came from two sources: either from the more evangelically inclined Quaker ministers from England, especially through the influence of Joseph John Gurney, or from the direct impact of Wesleyan revivalism following the Second Great Awakening of evangelical Christianity in America. Also, as Quakers moved westward they were increasingly influenced by the frontier revival meetings of traveling evangelists. These seemed exciting and spiritually nourishing compared with the very dull and lifeless quietistic practices in Quaker worship and ministry. This led to the adoption of a pastoral/programmed form of worship and ministry, which eventually led to the pastoral ministry and called for the training and recording of ministers of the Gospel to serve in the pastoral/programmed meetings. Many efforts were made during the next seventy-five years to formalize training for such leadership, but it was not until the establishment of the Earlham School of Religion in 1960 that a fully accredited Quaker seminary became available for such ministerial preparation.[20]

Today the following basic principles provide a guideline for ministry in worship:

1. Quaker ministry is prophetic; it is a calling of God and is ordained by God through the gift of the Holy Spirit. This call may be immediate and permanent, or it may be immediate and temporary.

2. Authority for ministry is from Christ through the Holy Spirit. It is not received by apostolic succession but by being in the same Spirit as the apostles were.

3. Ministry is given by a special empowerment and leading of the Holy Spirit. In this sense it is charismatic, exhibiting the gift and power of the Spirit at work in the life of the one who ministers.

4. Ministry takes place in the context of the church or meeting—the gathered community of believers and worshipers.

5. Ministry is not an office or profession but a response to the divine initiative with reference to the particular gifts of the person ministering. Recording of a minister is recognition by the meeting of a gift in the ministry. This is different from ordination of clergy in the mainline churches where authority and status are imparted, which Friends do not claim.

6. Ministry is freely given and freely received. This is what Friends mean by the "free Gospel ministry." All giving and support for ministry should be voluntary.

7. Ministry is universally possible for all believers. Everyone has a calling to ministry of some nature, although in many cases it may not be the vocal ministry. The "priesthood of all believers," as interpreted by Friends, universalizes all ministry and removes the distinction between clergy and laity.

8. Believers are called to specialized ministries based on specialized gifts of the persons called: e.g., teaching, preaching, pastoral care, counseling, administration, reconciling, eldering, clerking, and a variety of other roles of service to the meeting community.[21]

In 1960 Elton Trueblood wrote an important appraisal of ministry among Friends entitled "The Paradox of the Quaker Ministry."[22] Here he made a distinction between the "universal ministry" of every committed member of the meeting and the "specialized ministry" of those who are specially called to train and equip the general membership for their ministry. Friends in these specialized ministries cannot be classified as either clergy or laity, but instead represent a "third order" of persons who provide the specialized training and equipping needed. He cited Robert Barclay's Apology, (Proposition X, Article 26) as an authoritative basis for such an understanding of the Quaker ministry. This idea has come to have increasing acceptance and significance for Friends not only in the pastoral/programmed tradition but also in unprogrammed meetings where Friends are seeking ways to bring new life and vitality to their meetings.

Quaker Organization and Discipline

The Society of Friends began with a belief in the true church as spiritual, invisible, and beyond form and structure, but they were not able to hold strictly to this belief for long. Very early it became clear that a wholly spirit-centered theology and polity would be unable to deal with those within the Quaker fold who took liberties beyond the bounds of propriety. As soon as efforts were made to restrain such excesses, a debate arose between those who advocated complete freedom of the Spirit and those who felt the need for order and discipline. Thus arose, among others, the Wilkinson-Story controversy, which precipitated a division between those who believed the Spirit should be followed in every detail and those who held that the "Gospel order" called for both planning and disciplinary action against any who refused to abide by the recognized standards of the corporate body. The issue of the freedom of the individual in relationship to the common good of the meeting became a problem for Friends, and has continued to be a problem to this day. Throughout their history Friends have swung between antinomianism (bordering on anarchy) and a desire to establish disciplinary guidelines in both thought and behavior.

Because of discord in the Quaker ranks, in 1666 George Fox took the initiative, along with Richard Farnsworth and others, to organize monthly, quarterly, and yearly meetings. He set out to establish what he called a Gospel Order where "Christ is present in the midst of his people as ruler, governor and orderer." [23] Fox envisioned this as the order of the New Covenant of Jesus Christ, a divine, not an institutional, structure by means of which Christ would govern his church. Fox's expectation was that as members of the body sought the Light of Christ together they would be brought into a common sense of unity.

Although there are indications that the designation of elders occurred in the early 1650s, the recognition of elders (and later of overseers) as a formal church body did not come until the eighteenth century. The Society did not keep formal membership records until 1737, and then it was practiced primarily to determine the needs of those in physical want. Earlier, however, Friends had begun to keep records of births, deaths, marriages, and minutes of recommendation for those moving from one meeting to another. Corresponding with this organizational development was the formulation of Advices and Queries addressed to subordinate meetings. Again, these were initiated for the purpose of gathering important statistical information, but by the turn of the eighteenth century they began to give advice and formulate queries about matters of faith and practice, especially moral conduct. It was 1754 before a formal body of ministers and elders constituted a "select meeting," which meant that those not recognized as approved ministers and elders were not allowed to attend, including the overseers.

The elders were to make arrangements for meetings and to oversee the ministry and worship life of the meeting. This meant nurturing and encouraging Friends in the ministry, as well as determining who was acceptable as an "approved" minister. Overseers, who began to be recognized in the 1690s, held a separate function, which was the moral discipline and pastoral care of members. Both elders and overseers were guided by the growing body of material identified as Advices and Queries, and this constituted what becomes the first Discipline of the Religious Society of Friends. Because the elders and overseers were the guardians of the Discipline, they as a body became a kind of spiritual aristocracy. As time went on Friends increasingly felt the heavy hand of the elders and overseers who brought disownment procedures against individuals for not measuring up to the standard of the Discipline. In the latter part of the eighteenth century, for example, disownments for marrying out of meeting became very extensive. For a hundred years (1750-1850) the elders and overseers exercised their power and control as the Discipline was used to build what was called "a hedge" around the Society in order to keep Friends pure and undefiled from the world. The result was a steady loss of membership. Coupled with the quietistic turning inward mentioned earlier, this precipitated not only a decline but a "hardening of the arteries" of the Society which took two or more generations to overcome.

This entire episode has made Friends realize that while an invisible fellowship under the guidance of the Spirit may be something we all aspire to, it may indeed be an unreachable ideal. Some kind of balance has to be maintained between freedom and order, between individual liberty and the need for corporate decision-making and discipline, if a healthy state of accountability is to be achieved. Friends must realize that a certain level of organization, structure, and accountability is necessary if they are to enjoy the benefit of the religious values and testimonies which they espouse and cherish.

The Meeting for Business

The Quaker business procedure is one of the Society's unique practices and has become known as such by anyone who has any familiarity with Friends. To begin with, the business procedure, which deals with the practical affairs of the meeting, takes place in a meeting for worship, the assumption being that business is guided by the Spirit of Christ (or of God) just as worship is. Admittedly, Friends are not always faithful in seeking this together in the spirit of worship, but it is certainly the ideal to which they aspire. Much depends on the attitude of the worshipers, as well as the clerk, in determining how well this objective is achieved.

It has become popular in recent years to refer to the Quaker business procedure as a method for reaching decisions by consensus. This is misleading, however, for it implies that what happens is simply an accommodation of the wills of those gathered for decision-making. If this were all it is, then clearly it should not be called "a meeting for worship for the purpose of doing business." The historic understanding of the Quaker business method is that it is first of all a religious undertaking, even though the results involve practical matters. Friends have always insisted that there should not be a wall of separation between our relationship with God and our relationship with matters of everyday life. If our lives are in tune with the Spirit of God, then it is incumbent upon us to seek God's will in the practical affairs of our lives. This being the case, the task of the clerk in a Friends business meeting is to gather the "sense of the meeting" (rather than consensus)—what the members of the meeting discern to be the inward leading of the Spirit. And if all are seeking this Inward Light together, then surely they will be brought to a sense of unity, which the clerk can gather and record as the common leading of the meeting.

Gathering the sense of the meeting is quite different from gaining consensus, which attempts to accommodate conflicting wills and interests. It is true, however, that many times the latter is what actually takes place in a Friends meeting for business when members become involved in their own style of power politics and various individuals or groups end up jockeying for position to affect the outcome of a decision. Even though that need not happen where consensus is used in the best sense of the word, the fact is that it represents a political model misapplied to a spiritual process. Consensus is at heart a secular approach that defies the very theological foundations of Quaker faith and practice.

Another misconception of those who do not understand the Quaker business procedure is that unanimous consent must be given before a decision can be reached. This assumes a political model requiring that every person (i.e., every "vote") must be counted in the affirmative in order for the meeting to take action. What should happen in reaching a sense of the meeting is that if one or two, or even a few, persons do not feel in unity with the discernment of the majority, they may "stand aside," after making it clear to the group that although they do not agree with the decision, they are willing to trust the corporate judgment of the meeting. Then their consciences are free without having to hold up the decision-making process. On the other hand, meetings, and especially clerks, need to deal carefully and tenderly with minority views and leadings. Sometimes with the passage of time and changed circumstances minorities have been found to be right after all. As Friends seek the Light of Christ together in this manner, they will be brought into a common sense of the truth and the will of God regarding particular business matters and decisions.

Questions for Discussion

1. What is the distinction between "church" and "meeting" as far as Friends are concerned?
2. Compare the focus of Friends worship with that of Roman Catholics and Protestants.
3. What changes in the Society of Friends in the nineteenth century led to the pastoral/programmed form of worship and ministry?
4. To what extent has the problem of freedom and discipline (or freedom and order) plagued Friends throughout their history?
5. What are the Queries and Advices, and how did they arise in the history of Friends?
6. What is the difference between the clerk gathering "consensus" and "the sense of the meeting" in Quaker business procedure?

CHAPTER 7

Quakers
and the Sacraments

I f non-Quakers know anything about this "peculiar sect," as some would call the Friends, they probably know about their Peace Testimony, their use of silence in worship, and their testimony against the use of the sacraments. The latter, in particular, continues to be debated today by both Quakers and those who take issue with their position. It is a perennial issue in Friends' relationship with the National and World Councils of Churches, and the Quaker defense of their position has claimed much attention in the past. In Barclay's *Apology*, for example, two of his fifteen Propositions (chapters) are devoted to baptism and the Lord's Supper.

In the midst of all of this it is often forgotten that Friends believe in and practice the baptism of the Holy Spirit as well as holy (spiritual) communion in their worship. What they don't believe in is the efficacy of the outward elements—the use of bread, wine, and water in sacramental ceremonies of worship. Instead, Friends have formulated a sacramental theology that focuses on the "real Presence" in the act of worship. To take issue with this, it seems one would have to argue that the essence of the sacraments is centered in certain physical elements. But for a clearer understanding, let us examine in detail the meaning of sacrament and how Friends have differed from other Christians on this point.

The Meaning of Sacrament

In the fourth century Augustine defined a sacrament as a "visible sign of an invisible reality." Whenever the outward elements of the sacraments (bread, wine, and water) are used in Christian worship, the purpose is to celebrate as well as re-enact the life, death, and resurrection of Christ. The elements serve as signs to point us back to the original events where God met and engaged our humanity in the person of Jesus Christ for the purpose of salvation. Wherever liturgy, sacraments, and the preached Word are used in Christian worship, they focus on these past events.

Quakers aim to break through this mediatory and sacramental representation of the past in order that the worshiper may experience the *immediate* presence of Christ's grace, power, and transforming love. They hold that worship is only efficacious insofar as one touches and experiences God directly in the act, and no ceremonial re-enactment will suffice. If a sacrament is *where* God is present, then worship itself must become that sacramental event in which God is experienced.

Alan Kolp suggests that the sacraments are signs, indicators, or pointers to a faith experience that unites the worshiper with God. He says that Jesus should be understood as the "sign" of the invisible God. In this sense Jesus is the "primordial sacrament" because we believe that God was incarnate in Jesus Christ. If we as persons wish to become disciples of Christ, says Kolp, we also are called to become living signs of the invisible reality of God's presence. "The call to discipleship is not to participate in the sacraments, but to live sacramentally."[1]

We might put alongside this the often repeated phrase, "let your lives speak," allegedly spoken by George Fox in the seventeenth century and popularized by Elfrida Vipont Foulds in our own. The meaning implied is that our outward lives and behavior should be a sign of the Spirit of God working in us.[2]

Current Views

For more than three centuries Friends have proclaimed "the essentially spiritual nature of the believers' relationship to God."[3] For most, this has led to a testimony against the outward use of sacraments. Believing the inward way of the Spirit is not to be dependent upon rites, ceremonies, and liturgical aids, Friends maintain that "the presence of Christ in the midst" can be a living experience for all who open themselves to the Spirit of God. Growing out of this are three contemporary Quaker responses to the sacraments as they are traditionally celebrated in mainline churches.

1. First is the *impediment view*, which says that the sacraments are a hindrance to communion and worship. Because "Christ has come to teach his people himself," as George Fox declared, there is no way of improving on the reality of his presence through symbolic remembrances or re-enactments. Rather, believers should focus on the mystical presence of Christ in the moment of worship.

2. The *non-necessity view* holds that the sacraments are not efficacious as a means of grace and therefore are not necessary for worship or for personal reconciliation with God. Because the sacraments are "shadows," not the "real presence," their symbolic representations may be helpful to some in worship but are not necessary. As to whether or not one should partake of the sacraments, the advice is, "Let your conscience be your guide." Those who find them helpful should not be condemned, but "there is a more excellent way" to experience the reality of God.

3. The third response we shall call the *Friends view re-examined* , of which there are three variations.

a) Ever since David Updegraff and members of Ohio (Damascus) Yearly Meeting (now Evangelical Friends Church Eastern Region) asked that the ordinances be introduced into Friends worship in the 1880s, there has been limited practice of baptism and communion in that Yearly Meeting.[4] Updegraff made his case on biblical grounds and pled for freedom of conscience to practice the ordinances. More recently this same view has been claimed elsewhere among Friends on the grounds that baptism and communion are desired by some and that nothing in Scripture or Friends doctrine forbids their practice.

b) A systematic and persuasive case was made several years ago by the British Friend, Maurice Creasey, calling for re-examination of the historic Quaker position on baptism and the Lord's Supper, together with a fresh exegesis of the pertinent Scripture. Creasey was concerned that if Friends held too narrow a view on this issue it would only serve to impede ecumenical unity. He asserted that he "would be entirely misunderstood if. . . [his statement] were regarded as a plea for Friends to 'adopt the Sacraments.'" However, he warned against becoming "'frozen' into an attitude of protest which had little relevance. . . . The questions it is desired to raise are whether Baptism and the Supper, understood as in the New Testament, need be excluded from our corporate experience and practice and whether, if practiced, they could not be experienced as complementary to our mode of gathered, waiting worship."[5]

c) There are a few Friends, affiliated for the most part with unprogrammed meetings, who find it helpful to participate occasionally in liturgical services and sacraments. An example of this is the person who reportedly was refused membership in a Friends meeting because she simultaneously celebrated the Eucharist in a nearby place of worship.

Perhaps this phenomenon has some affinity with a practice in Philadelphia where for years there was occasional crossing over in membership between the Episcopalians and Friends, depending on one's satisfaction or dissatisfaction with high church or low church forms of worship.

Historical Roots

Some believe that the early Quaker view of the sacraments "arose in a corporate experience which was then given biblical and theological justification."[6] Rather than using the Bible as an "encyclopedic handbook" for faith and practice, Friends begin with the experience of the living Christ. Thus to debate the sacraments on the basis of whether Jesus instituted baptism and the Lord's Supper is only part of the Quaker rationale. So let us look at both the biblical and extra-biblical reasons for their objection to the sacraments.

George Fox and early Friends believed that outward forms, rites, and ceremonies of religion belonged to the old Jewish covenant and that Jesus came to initiate a new covenant, spiritually based and unencumbered by ritual, ceremony and symbolism (see Eph., 2:15; Col. 2:14; Heb. 2:1-10). As followers of Christ they were called to what Rufus Jones referred to as "a religion of life and faith" and not "a new form of legalism and ordinances." Hence, Christ supersedes the old law and cultic practices of the Hebrew people and opens up a new way to God.[7]

Friends did not find the sacraments of baptism and the Lord's Supper explicitly commanded by Christ. In defense of this view Henry Cadbury quotes a 1944 Friends' Discipline: Friends "do not find that Jesus commanded that the 'sacraments' be observed as perpetual ordinances of his Church."[8] At the same time Friends used Scripture to support their testimony against the sacraments. Because of this, Maurice Creasey has presented a challenge to traditional Quaker interpretation: "I propose to ask . . . whether the biblical exegesis relied upon by Friends with remarkable uniformity throughout the Society's history really proves what it has always been held to prove."[9]

In order to consider this, we must examine the biblical basis of the Friends' position on baptism and the Lord's Supper.

Baptism

Friends believe that the true form of baptism for all who enter the new life in Christ is the baptism of the Holy Spirit. They hold that John's baptism with water was superseded by Jesus' baptism with the Holy Spirit and with fire (Matt. 3:11).[10] Although Jesus himself was baptized (Matt. 3:13-16), there is no report of his baptizing others (John 4:2). The Great Commission in Matthew 28:19 calls for baptism of new converts in the name of the Father, Son, and Holy Spirit, but some point out that this Trinitarian reference occurs only in Matthew and that there is no record of its actual use in New Testament times. However, there are several references to baptism in the name of Jesus (Acts 2:38; 8:16; 10:48; 19:5; 22:16), and the baptism in Matthew 28:19 could very well refer to baptism with the Spirit rather than water.

It seems significant that the apostle Paul reports performing only a few baptisms and justifies this by declaring: "Christ did not send me to baptize but to preach the gospel" (1 Cor. 1:14-17). But more important for Friends are instances where water baptism is indicated as unnecessary. When Cornelius was baptized (Acts 10:44-48), the gift of the Holy Spirit preceded the rite of water baptism, suggesting that water was not a precondition of baptism by the Spirit. Friends also point to the thief who was crucified with Jesus. There is no report of him being baptized, which suggests that he was able to enter the kingdom without receiving baptism in any formal way.

In a study of George Fox and the sacraments, T. Canby Jones concludes that Fox "actually believed in only one Sacrament, that of being engrafted into Christ . . . . Though he speaks of both baptism and the Lord's Supper, he spiritualizes them into essentially the same thing . . . . Now that Christ the substance has come all types and shadows of him are of no more use." [11]

Thus, Friends stress the inward way of the Spirit as the pathway to the reality of God rather than outward ceremonies and rites. It is important to emphasize again, however, that Friends do believe in baptism and communion even though they reject the sacramental elements. Rufus Jones writes: "They [Friends] claimed that true baptism is a cleansing and purifying process by which the believer enters into the life and death of Christ, and rises with Him in newness of spirit and power. In like manner the true communion is a joyous partaking of Christ as the bread of life, and an immediate consciousness of His real Presence, spirit meeting with Spirit."[12] This leads us then to a consideration of the Lord's Supper.

The Lord's Supper

The biblical injunction reported by Paul in 1 Corinthians 11:24-25, "Do this in remembrance of me," was presumably spoken by Jesus at the Last Supper. If Jesus did give this commandment to his disciples, one would assume that the writers of the Gospels would have reported it; yet it is recorded only in Luke 22:19-20. And the fact that these verses do not appear in the earliest manuscripts and are no longer included in most of the newer translations leads to speculation that the sacramental rite of the Lord's Supper was instituted by the early church rather than by Jesus. [13]

A second thing to note is that at the very point where the sharing of the loaf and cup appears in the Matthew, Mark, and Luke accounts of

Jesus' last meal with his disciples, the Gospel of John substitutes Jesus' footwashing of the disciples; and John clearly reports that Jesus commanded his disciples to do likewise in the future. In light of these observations Friends have held that Jesus did not intend to institute a sacramental rite at the Last Supper; or, if he intended such a memorial at all, they believe it was to be spiritually interpreted and should take place whenever the followers of Jesus come together in a fellowship meal. Friends also point out that the Last Supper was in all probability a Jewish Passover meal and was not intended as a permanent memorial. In his study of the sacraments, Edward Grubb, a British Quaker, writes:

> There is no evidence that the Eucharistic ceremony can be traced to the mind of Jesus Himself. If the Church's authority is all that can be claimed for it, the observance can no longer be based on a plain command of the Lord.[14]

Because Friends strongly emphasize the spiritual nature of the sacraments, it is important to understand how they came to this conclusion in the case of the Lord's Supper. Gerald K. Hibbert gives this clear and concise explanation:

> Although . . . the author of the Fourth Gospel makes no mention of the Bread and Wine at the Last Supper, he leaves us in no doubt as to the spiritual reality underlying the eating and drinking thereof. In his sixth chapter he gives us a deeply satisfying conception of what true communion with Christ involves. "He that eateth my flesh and drinketh my blood abideth (dwelleth) with me, and I in him . . . . It is the spirit that quickeneth; the flesh profiteth nothing; the words that I have spoken unto you are spirit, and are life." Could anything be plainer or more emphatic

. . . . He deliberately omits all mention of the bread and wine, and fastens instead on their inner underlying meaning, the spiritual union with that Christ whose "flesh is meat indeed, and whose blood is drink indeed." [15]

Revelation 3:20 was another important passage that early Friends quoted in order to make clear their spiritual understanding of the Lord's Supper: "Behold, I stand at the door and knock; if any one hears my voice and opens the door, I will come in to him and eat with him, and he with me."

It is also noteworthy that there are no references to the Lord's Supper in the epistle to the Romans (chapters 1-8), which is sometimes referred to as the "Gospel According to Paul." Neither is there reference to the Supper in 1 John nor in the Pastoral Epistles, which deal with the life and work of the local church.

The Sacramental View

In the twentieth century Friends have developed the testimony about the sacramental view of all life, maintaining that it is not just in special sacramental events (such as baptism and communion) that we experience the grace of God, but that all occasions of life and every meal have the potential to become sacred means of God's grace. This view is similar to that of William Temple, the British clergyman-theologian, who has written about the sacramental view of the universe in his classic work, *Nature, Man and God*. By way of interpreting this view, Elton Trueblood says:

Quakers do not intend, and never intended, to establish a merely spiritual religion. Quakers take so seriously the idea that ours is a sacramental universe that they cannot limit the notion to a particular ceremony or initiation. . . . How many sacraments are there? There are seventy times seven. [16]

At the turn of the century John Wilhelm Rowntree emphasized the same view when he wrote: "For all experience is a holy baptism, a perpetual supper with the Lord, and all of life a sacrifice, holy and acceptable unto God."[17] This concept of the sacramental view of life also coincides with the Quaker testimony that there are no uniquely sacred times (days) or places; instead, all of life has the possibility of becoming an outward sign of an inward grace.

Friends' testimony against the outward sacraments was also in keeping with their earlier rejection of artistic symbolism, in the form of music and art, as a means of expressing religious reality. Such sensory expressions were considered creaturely activity aimed at appealing to the eye and ear and were not grounded in the Spirit. Most Friends today accept the arts, but they make the distinction that music and art are aids to worship whereas baptism and communion are celebrated as means of grace and are regarded by some traditions as necessary for salvation.

Finally, it should be noted that the word "sacrament" is not a biblical term. You cannot look it up in a concordance. According to a study done by Dean Freiday, the Latin *sacramentum* is a translation of the Greek *musterion*, which means "secret." This term is used twenty-seven times in the New Testament but is never applied to baptism or the Eucharist. *Sacramentum* is derived, says Freiday, from pagan religion and culture and first appears in the writings of Tertullian in the middle of the third century when he refers to the Eucharist as a sacrament. When the term comes to be applied to baptism and the Lord's Supper in general, they are considered religious rites rather than efficacious means of grace for salvation.[18]

It is speculated that the Greek mystery cults lay behind the sacramental idea of initiation and participation in the life of a hero-god. While this may not be a valid argument against sacraments today, Friends point out that historically superstition and magic were sometimes associated with the sacraments and thus have made them suspect as authentic forms of Christian worship. For example, early in the second century Ignatius referred to the Lord's Supper as "the medicine of immortality," and a century later Tertullian referred to baptism as "the medicinal bath of regeneration." Although modern-day sacramentalists and liturgists evidence little of this kind of association, it is part of the reason Friends have been opposed to the sacraments.

However, Friends' view of the sacraments is not without its own dangers and inconsistencies. For example, if we spiritualize the Christian faith too much, we court the dangers of Docetism, Manichaeism, and Gnosticism, all of which were heretical doctrines in the early church. Also, modern Quaker emphasis on the sacramental view of all life may border on pantheism and sometimes fails to deal with the problem of evil in the world. It is simply not true that all of life is sacred and therefore sacramental, although Friends would claim that it has the potential to become so. Or, Friends may so emphasize the spiritual that they underestimate the historical nature of Christian faith and thus over-spiritualize religion and life. This reminds one of the well-worn aphorism: "If you become too other-worldly (too spiritual) you are no earthly good!"

Friends and the Ecumenical Movement

In this century Friends have often joined in the ecumenical interests of the church. Not all are associated with the various councils of churches, but such affiliations have been strong in England and North

America. Friends support the ecumenical movement at many points, but there are also areas of difference in theology that cannot be ignored, especially with respect to the sacraments. In recent years there has been a strong effort to find grounds for Christian unity on the basis of "One Baptism, One Eucharist and a Mutually Recognized Ministry."[19] The issue was brought to a head for Friends at the Fifth Assembly of the World Council of Churches in 1975, when the assembly amended both the World Council's Constitution and its Faith and Order By-Laws "to call the churches to the goal of visible unity in one faith and in one eucharistic fellowship."[20] To expect member churches to achieve "visible unity" in "one eucharistic fellowship" seemed to exclude both Friends and the Salvation Army, which holds a similar view of the sacraments. In response, the Friends General Conference voiced their objection; and subsequently the Friends United Meeting presented the following statement, which was adopted by the FUM General Board in March of 1980.

We reaffirm the Friends' testimony to the essentially spiritual nature of the believer's relationship to God through Jesus Christ in the Holy Spirit. The Inward Way of the Spirit is not dependent upon specific visible signs. Because we believe that Christ himself has come to teach His people, any outward sign may become a hindrance to experiencing the presence and grace of God. It is only the living presence of Christ that is efficacious for reconciliation with God. The visible sign of that living presence is the faithful and obedient Church.

The Church consists of those gathered by and in the power and presence of Christ and is a spiritual union with Christ and with one another in the covenant life in Christ. This visible unity of the

Church is found in the fellowship of those who love Christ and who love each other. "A new commandment I give to you; that you love one another; even as I have loved you, that you also love one another." (John 13:34-35 RSV) In relation to the Church, Christ is Lord, Savior, Priest, Prophet, Teacher, and Comforter. Wherever these ministries of Christ are experienced in the presence of one another we have a true Christian fellowship. With or without sacramental rites, such experience is the heart of Christian worship.[21]

Friends have a unique view of the sacraments, which needs to be understood by other Christians. At the same time, Friends should reaffirm to the Christian churches of the world their belief that unity will not be achieved through common belief and practice about the sacraments. Rather, Christian unity will be achieved through a common loyalty to Christ and the Holy Spirit, expressed through the visible sign of Christ's church, the fellowship of believers, made manifest through their love for one another.

Questions for Discussion

1. What is the meaning of "sacrament" and how has it been important in Christian worship?
2. Why do Friends object to ceremonialism and symbolism in worship?
3. On what basis have Friends not found baptism and communion ordained by Jesus?
4. What is the meaning of the Quaker idea of "the sacramental view of life"?

(continued)

---

5. Have Friends made too big an issue of the nonuse of sacraments in worship? Explain your answer.
6. In what sense are the testimonies sacramental for Friends?

CHAPTER 8

The Quaker Testimonies

"Quakerism is a way of life." This saying, common among Friends, is intended to make it clear that Quakerism is not just a set of beliefs or a statement of faith; it is a practical, ethical, and functional religious approach to life. That is to say, it is a religious faith to be lived out and not just professed and talked about. This is not to suggest that Friends do not regard faith commitment as primary and prerequisite to action. Indeed, our first responsibility is to seek the truth in terms of God's will. But after we have discerned it, we are obliged to carry out the will of God by "doing the truth." The inward journey of faith can never be separated from the outward journey of practice, and Friends believe the two are integral and indispensable to each other.

Plainness and Self-Denial

Early Friends believed that commitment to the Christ Within would bear fruit in their outward lives and "testify" to the truth of their inward experience. In this way they bore witness to their Christian faith. William Penn believed that the Christian life meant becoming "followers of the perfect Jesus, that most heavenly man."[1] George Fox, Robert Barclay, and William Penn all agreed about what the new life in Christ entailed, and it stemmed from their belief that "evil begins from within, and not from without."[2] Thus to be a disciple of Christ one must follow the injunctions of Jesus: "If any man would come after me, let him deny himself and take up his cross and follow me" (Matt. 16:24). Penn declared that "the cares and pleasures of this life choke and destroy the seed of the Kingdom, and quite hinder all progress in the hidden and divine life."[3] George Fox's *Epistle No. 250* was devoted entirely to warning Friends to "keep out of the vain fashions of the world." He admonished them to "keep all in modesty and plainness, fervency and sincerity and be circumspect . . . take heed of the world's fashions, lest you be moulded up into their spirit." They were to "mind the hidden man of the heart, which is a meek and quiet spirit, which is of great price to the Lord."[4] For Friends this meant a life ("the way") of plainness and self-denial and the avoidance of vain and empty customs.

William Penn dealt at great length with the way of plainness and self-denial in his famous volume, *No Cross, No Crown*, and Robert Barclay closed his *Apology* with Proposition 15, which spelled out his call for holiness and integrity in daily life. His preamble to the Proposition provides a good summary of what it meant to early Quakers to be committed to Christ:

> The chief purpose of all religion is to redeem men from the spirit and vain pursuits of this world, and to lead them into inward communion with God. All vain and empty customs and habits, whether of word or deed, should be rejected by those who have come to fear the Lord.

Taking one's hat off to another person, bowing or cringing, and the other similar foolish and superstitious formalities which accompany them, should be forsaken. All of these were invented to feed man's pride through the vain pomp and glory of this world.

Theatrical productions which are not beneficial, frivolous recreation, sports and games which waste precious time and divert the mind from the witness of God in the heart, should be given up. Christians should have a living sense of reverence for God, and should be leavened with the evangelical Spirit which leads into sobriety, gravity, and godly fear. When we abide in these, the blessing of the Lord is felt to attend us in the necessary occupations by which we gain sustenance for the outward man. [5]

It is instructive that when Barclay begins to spell out the testimonies embodied in this Proposition some of the results sound familiar to us today, while others seem a bit strange. He is clear about the testimony against "revenge and war," which we would call the peace testimony. He declares a testimony against swearing and oath taking, which we would call the testimony of telling the truth. He denounces "flattering titles", "kneeling and bowing," which suggest a testimony of equality. But he also has a testimony against "vain displays" and "superfluous" wearing apparel. He speaks out against sports, recreation and plays which do not honor God. If Friends must have "diversion," he suggests "reading history," "serious conversation," "gardening," or "geometrical and mathematical exercises." Some of these may sound dull and forbidding but they constituted for early Friends a life of plainness and self-denial, which they believed Christian discipleship required.

Meaning of the Testimonies

What is it about this ethical dimension of Quakerism that makes their testimonies so important? To understand this, we must begin by defining what Friends mean by "testimonies." A testimony is an outward expression of an inward leading of the Spirit, or an outward sign of what Friends believe to be an inward revelation of truth. It is no coincidence that this sounds familiar following our discussion of the Quaker sacramental view of life in the previous chapter, for the testimonies have a sacramental quality for Friends. They are an outward expression of an inward spiritual discernment, constituting faith incarnated in action. The testimonies provide the moral and ethical fruits of one's inward life of the Spirit. To quote Worth Hartman, "They arise more out of a concern for purity, holiness, consistency with divine order than from a passion for social justice."[6] In a very real sense the testimonies are the Quaker "articles of faith" translated into action. In the final analysis they are the Quaker equivalent of a creed.

Frequently Friends speak of Quaker values, a term that Friends of an earlier period probably would not have understood. In fact, there is a great deal of talk today, particularly in academic circles, about "values" and "value commitments," which constitute a secular way of talking about religion and faith commitments. Usually these refer to rationally determined goals held up as ideals toward which we strive. Quakers prefer to use the term "testimonies" rather than "values" when speaking about our basic principles of faith and practice so we do not run the risk of secularizing our terminology. Our testimonies are clearly rooted in our religious faith and experience and are not just rational projections, or what earlier Friends might have called "notional religion."

Although the purpose of this chapter is to discuss the Quaker social testimonies, it is the Quaker religious testimonies that lie behind our social testimonies—for example, the Friends' testimony about the individual's direct relationship with God, or the testimony about the sacramental nature of life, or the testimony about personal integrity and truth-telling. These religious or spiritual testimonies of the soul undergird and form the basis for Friends' social testimonies and cannot be overlooked when considering the social application of the Quaker faith. Thus much of this book so far can constitute a religious prologue to this treatment of the social testimonies of Friends.

Philosophy and History of the Friends Testimonies

Believing that life is not what it ought to be and that it needs to be transformed, Quakers have always had a passion for making the world over. Since the time of George Fox, Friends have had a deep sense that one ought to be able to live as if the kingdom of God were a reality here and now and not some golden age of the past or some blessed event of the future. Along with a drive for Christian perfection in one's personal life (described in chapter 5), there must be a corresponding drive for Christian perfection in the corporate, social, and political world. The Peace Testimony is an affirmation and hope that war can be done away with, as is the belief that evil, disorder, and injustice in other areas of society can be replaced with a new order of God's commonwealth. Friends are indebted to their Puritan forebears, who were influenced by John Calvin, for their belief that this world is ultimately accountable to God's order and design. What this means is that this world can be transformed by the grace of God, coupled with the industry and ingenuity of human beings. Fox and early Quakers went even further, concluding that the whole cosmos could be redeemed and made over into the image of God! This is not a Pollyannaish outlook nor sentimental optimism but a profound belief in the power of God to prevail over the forces of sin and evil in the world and in all creation. Thus Friends' appeal for ethical purity is cosmic in scope.

At the turn of the century John Wilhelm Rowntree uttered a now-famous prayer that perfectly describes the mood and passion of the Quakers: "[Oh Christ] lay on us the burden of the world's suffering and drive us forth with the apostolic fervor of the early Church."[7] When one makes even a cursory review of the history of Friends' involvement and work in philanthropic, peace, and social concerns, one must stand amazed at the incredible extent to which a group so small numerically has been involved in ministering to the ills and needs of the world. The list is both impressive and far-reaching: education, prison reform, religious freedom, abolition of slavery, Indian work, care of the poor and the insane, capital punishment, temperance, war and famine relief, peace and service work, women's rights, economic and racial justice, ecological concerns, and the list goes on and on. Also, Friends became involved in business, industry, and commerce not just for personal gain but to provide quality goods and services at an equitable price to the consumer and to improve the working and living conditions of laborers. The history of Quaker philanthropy is an exhilarating story. (See Chapter 10, "Quaker Mission, Service, and Outreach.")[8]

Social testimonies undergird all of this concern to improve the conditions of people and to make over the social order to better serve human need. Not surprisingly, the social testimonies of today are not the same as they were in the seventeenth century. In that early period there was a testimony against paying tithes to the established church, a testimony against taking oaths (swearing) in courts of law, a testimony against wars and fighting, a testimony against using titles—to express their concern for equality, a testimony against "hat honor"— bowing before superiors. There were testimonies about "plain" language and dress and about simplicity in the furnishing of Quaker homes. These and other testimonies gave expression to the burning concerns of the day.

For the most part these testimonies appeared in the form of Advices and Queries to those who claimed identification with Friends. By 1738 they were included in a *Book of Extracts*, which in time became a *Book of Discipline for Friends*. By 1783 the Discipline was published for wider circulation among the meetings and individuals. During the eighteenth century the Discipline dealt primarily with matters of moral conduct as well as practical advices and testimonies for Friends. Not until the nineteenth century did the Discipline become doctrinal in content. Whether moral, practical or doctrinal, however, the Discipline was all too often used as a narrow and restrictive test for membership, so that it became the source of much controversy and eventually one of the reasons for the Separations of Friends in the first half of the nineteenth century.

The Social Testimonies Today

While the testimonies expressed today are clearly linked with the past, in some instances they have been updated to fit the needs of changing times. For example, payment of tithes to the established church is not an issue now, although payment of war taxes has become an issue in relationship to military defense and preparation for war. Also, concern about ecological matters today is rapidly becoming a new testimony as there is an increasing awareness of the pollution, erosion, and destruction of our environment, all of which drastically affects the realm of nature so essential to our survival as human beings. Given this background, let us now take a closer look at the main social testimonies of the Religious Society of Friends.

Integrity

The call for honesty lies at the heart of Quakerism. It is a testimony rooted in the Quaker respect for truthfulness. The early Quakers were known as "Friends of Truth" and "Publishers of Truth," and "Truth" with a capital "T" was a very special word in their vocabulary. Respect for this kind of integrity calls for a correspondence between what one professes and how one translates that into action in real life. Cecil Hinshaw, who has written impressively on early Friends and the testimonies, writes: "The essence of early Quakerism is precisely in a demand for complete integrity of the individual in . . . relation to God, to other people, and to oneself."[9] He further notes the close parallel between the Quaker commitment to integrity and the search for perfection. Both call for ethical purity prompted by obedience to the Light of Christ Within.

Hinshaw points to one of George Fox's early encounters, at age nineteen, to illustrate his deep sense of integrity. Fox had gone to a fair on some business and was invited to drink beer with two men who professed the faith (i.e., Christians). At first he joined with them, but soon they began to "drink healths" to each other and offered the challenge that the one who stopped first would pay for the drinks. At this point Fox, as he recorded in his *Journal*, "was grieved that any that made profession of religion should offer to do so." He paid for his drink and returned home. That night he could not sleep because of his stricken conscience over the behavior of professed Christians. In his wrestling with the Lord he made a commitment to separate himself from the kind of vanity he had experienced at the drinking bout.[10] Commenting on this incident, Cecil Hinshaw says:

> George Fox cannot be understood apart from a recognition that the driving force of his life at this time was for complete integrity.

With a passion that defied logic he demanded for himself and for others a life of holy obedience in even the smallest details of life.[11]

Another early dimension and manifestation of the testimony of integrity had to do with Friends' concern for honesty and truth-telling in their public life and in their business dealings. Believing that the price set should not exceed the value and that they should then stick to the stated price rather than bargain, Quakers became known for their single price system.

The testimony of integrity was most severely tested, however, when Friends refused to take oaths in the courts. They did this for two reasons: first, the biblical injunction not to swear at all but "let your communication be, Yea, yea; Nay, nay: for whatsoever is more than these cometh of evil" (Matt. 5:37 KJV; see also Matt. 5:33-37 and James 5:12);[12] and second, (the reason cited more often today) the oath implied a double standard of truth and suggested that part of the time they told lies. Quakers believed they should tell the truth all the time and not just when asked to take an oath. It is difficult now to fully appreciate the price those early Friends had to pay in order to maintain this testimony of integrity, for their refusal to take the oath resulted in suffering and imprisonment.

Simplicity

This testimony carried the Quaker perfectionist ethic a step further, applying it to daily life. In this regard early Friends were admonished to shun ornamentation in personal dress and grooming as well as in the furnishing of their houses. William Penn's *No Cross, No Crown* became a kind of Quaker handbook advising Friends about their manner of living. Today this testimony of simplicity is often used in reference to our undisciplined life-styles, suggesting a manner and standard of living that avoids superfluity and excess. The same may also apply to eating habits and to the use of tobacco, alcohol, and drugs, which can undermine both the health and the life of holy obedience.

Another application of the testimony is the use of time and the simplification of one's schedule—namely, the matter of priorities and how we arrange them. The tendency is to overburden ourselves with the amount of work we try to do. Matthew 6:22 is instructive here: "The light of the body is the eye: if therefore thine eye be single, thy whole body shall be full of light" (KJV). The life of simplicity is the focused, disciplined life in which we do not take on more than we can reasonably handle. This means uncomplicating our overscheduled and overburdened lives. It means having a clear sense of what is most important and learning how to leave aside those things that detract from and clutter up our lives—the excess baggage. In short, the testimony of simplicity calls for a reordering of our lives so that we become spiritually centered and focused.

Simplicity does not necessarily mean a life of voluntary poverty, but it does mean that we become good stewards of all that we have and that we become sensitive to the needs of others. John Woolman speaks to this when he says: "To turn all the treasures we possess into the channel of universal love becomes the business of our lives."[13]

Peace

This is the central testimony of the Religious Society of Friends. Friends the world over are recognized for their peace witness, and they, along with the Mennonites and Church of the Brethren, constitute the three Historic Peace Churches.

In the beginning of the Society of Friends the Peace Testimony was not fully developed, but emerged over a period of nearly ten years. Although those who became identified with the Quaker movement often fought in Cromwell's army in the English Civil War, by the time

Charles II was restored to the throne in 1660 Friends were becoming clear about their commitment to peace. This was reflected in their first corporate statement, which was addressed to the king in 1661. It was a time of persecution of Dissenter groups, including the Friends, and because they were sometimes confused with the Fifth Monarchy Men, who advocated violence, they were often jailed. It was in response to these circumstances that they issued a public statement, which read in part:

> We do testify to the world that the Spirit of Christ which leads us into all truth, will never move us to fight and war against any man with outward weapons, neither for the Kingdom of Christ nor for the kingdoms of this world.[14]

Because Friends place such emphasis on the dignity and worth of the individual, perhaps best expressed in George Fox's famous phrase, "that of God in every one," it is commonly assumed today that this forms the cornerstone of the Friends Peace Testimony.[15] Although that claim in itself may be true, it is too simplistic a statement, and it was not where Friends began in the seventeenth century. Again we refer to the work Cecil Hinshaw has done to show that the Friends testimonies were rooted in their search for Christian perfection. He points out that the modern emphasis on the sacredness of the individual was not a major emphasis of early Friends. Commenting on this, he says:

> Although Quakers later came to a more absolute position, in the first ten years or so of Quakerism there was not a clear testimony on the matter of taking human life because of the sacredness of such life as the creation of God. Yet they quite generally refused to fight. The apparent inconsistency is explained when we see it

was the violence, the hate, the selfishness inevitably involved in fighting that bothered them. Fox was perhaps even more concerned with what violence did to the one who used it than he was with the results of the violence on the person against whom it was directed. This is apparent in his classic and often-quoted words: "I told them I knew from whence all wars arose, even from the lusts, according to James' doctrine; and that I lived in the virtue of that life and power that took away the occasion of all wars."[16]

These words formed Fox's response when he was asked by the civil authorities to accept a commission in the army. After telling them that he "lived in the virtue of that life and power that took away the occasion of all wars," he added: "I told them I was come into the covenant of peace which was before wars and strife were." [17] This further confirms that Fox's refusal to fight began as an inward conviction and not because of outward pragmatic arguments.

What, then, are the reasons for the Friends Peace Testimony? On this issue, as he did with many others, Fox began with a direct revelation or "opening": bearing arms was wrong and his conscience, enlightened by the divine Light of Christ, would not allow him to take up weapons to fight. Following close upon this direct inward revelation, Fox gave biblical reasons for his peace witness.

Howard Brinton, in an excellent pamphlet, *The Peace Testimony of the Society of Friends*, cites a number of New Testament passages to show that Fox's peace position was well grounded in Scripture, and more particularly in the teachings of Jesus: "Love your enemies"; "Blessed are the peacemakers"; "Resist not evil"; "Whosoever smiteth thee on thy right cheek turn to him the other also"; "All they that take up the sword shall perish with the sword"; "If my kingdom were of this world then would my servants fight."[18] Thus, Quakers believed that the way of the cross of Jesus was entirely inconsistent with war or preparation for it.

Other reasons for the Peace Testimony have to do with Friends' concern about what the spirit of violence would do to their souls as well as their concern about preserving "that of God" in other persons. Friends also believe in the positive power of love and reconciliation to overcome evil and bring about peace and justice; they believe in the transformation not only of individuals, but of the whole world. Their doctrine of perfection has led them to envision the possibility of a "peaceable kingdom," which constitutes a concept of "holy worldliness." It was this which motivated William Penn to declare that "true godliness don't turn men out of the world, but enables them to live better in it, and excites their endeavors to mend it."[19]

Finally, Friends reason on pragmatic grounds that war does not pay. Its destructiveness almost invariably leaves both winners and losers dispirited and in disarray. The legacy of every war is a new set of problems that can easily sow the seeds for still another war. Somehow this vicious cycle needs to be broken, which must become the ever-present concern for Quaker peace-workers.

What hope is there that Friends can achieve these goals of peace and reconciliation? Does the Peace Testimony have any practical application, or is it an unattainable dream? Some years ago Benjamin Seaver wrote an article for *The Friend*, entitled "Three Definitions of Peace," in which he gave some practical suggestions about ways we can effectively work for peace.[20] He spelled out three levels of peacemaking where we need to apply ourselves, all of which are important and deserve a commitment of our efforts. (1) The first is working for "peace as an inner spiritual state," which aims to produce personal serenity and tranquility of the spirit, mind, and conscience. This calls for a spiritual transformation on our part. (2) The second is working for "peace as the absence of conflict." This can be achieved on a family and local community level where we develop one-to-one relationships with each other. Although human conflict resulting from personal self-interest may never be entirely eliminated at this level, Seaver believes that a degree of accommodation and harmony can be reached that will prevent conflict from breaking into violence. (3) The third level, what Seaver calls "peace as public order and security," is made possible by law enforcement, punishing those who disrupt the peace. Persons do not have to be saints to function amicably at this level of peacekeeping. While the first two options will not prevent war, says Seaver, the latter can. Thus he wants to convince Friends of the importance of working at the third level to avoid our mutual destruction as human beings. But he also stresses the importance of working at all three levels if we are to experience peace and harmony in all areas of life. Although many Friends who uphold the Peace Testimony would not concur with Seaver's third level of working for peace, it does provide an example of how Friends try to be concrete and constructive in their peacemaking. The Peace Testimony is not just a negative objection to participation in war; it is a positive attempt to establish the conditions of peace.

Equality

From the beginning equality has been an important social testimony of Friends. In the seventeenth century they were ahead of their time in recognizing the rights and gifts of women in the affairs of the church, school, and home. They were not perfect in this respect, but they made a good start. Very early Friends also demonstrated concern for justice and equal rights for native Americans; for the care of the insane; for the treatment of prisoners; and for the needs of the poor. In the eighteenth century they were at least a generation ahead of others in the freeing of their slaves and were zealous abolitionists.

Quakers have always opposed the use of titles in addressing other persons, and part of their reason for the "plain language" (in particular the use of "thee" and "thou") was that they not honor one person over another. Their refusal to doff their hats or bow before persons of honor, wealth, and authority represented their testimony to the equality of all persons before God. Everyone was believed to be precious in the sight of God because everyone was created in the image of God. In the twentieth century this same concept has been expressed in the phrase "that of God in every one," which we have indicated before was Fox's way of declaring the worth and dignity, as well as the divine capacity, present in all persons.

In reviewing the social testimonies it is difficult to know what to include and what to omit. It is clear that the testimonies already mentioned (integrity, simplicity, peace, and equality) constitute the central Quaker testimonies in our day. Howard Brinton would include still another: community, which reflects Friends' sense that they are members one of another and that Quakerism is not just individualism.[21] It also reflects their concern for the needs of other people in the world and the belief that we are not islands unto ourselves, but are all God's children and must be accountable to one another in looking after the needs of our sisters and brothers regardless of class, race, religion, or national origin. The testimony of community might also include our concern for the environment, for the world of nature is part of God's creation and needs to be preserved by good stewardship practices. There is also growing concern about sexist language (which implies male dominance over women) and about the rights of persons of homosexual orientation. It must be noted, however, that Friends are by no means united on some of these concerns, including the rights of the unborn versus the mother's right to choose in abortion cases.

The bottom line of the testimonies is consistency: a consistent correspondence between what we believe and how our beliefs get translated into action, which carries us back full circle to the testimony of integrity. If Friends are true to their basic faith commitments, then it naturally follows that they have to live out their faith in practical ways that not only affect them personally but affect all the human family and the whole created world.

Do Friends put into practice what they teach about the social testimonies? That is the final question. Clearly some are more conscientious than others, so the record of performance is not always consistent. It needs to be pointed out, however, that in the history of the Society of Friends there have always been the "absolutists" and the "relativists," to use the terminology of Frederick Tolles in his excellent chapter on the history of Friends involvement in political life.[22] Tolles cites George Fox as an example of the absolutist position in his relationship to the English authorities in the 1650s, comparing him to William Penn who represented the relativist position because his instrumentality in establishing the Pennsylvania "Holy Experiment" sometimes required political compromise. "Between these two poles Quaker political attitudes and behavior have oscillated" throughout Friends' history.[23] Likewise, Friends have not always been consistent in their response to the ethical imperatives of the Quaker social testimonies. Most would agree, nevertheless, that they are the goals to which Friends generally aspire and are committed, and Friends are often admonished to remain faithful in living out these testimonies in daily life.

Questions for Discussion

1. What is meant by the statement, "Quakerism is a way of life"?
2. What is a Friends testimony?
3. What difference is there, if any, between Quaker testimonies and what are often referred to as Quaker principles or values?
4. What is the difference, if any, between Quaker religious and social testimonies?
5. Why have Friends objected to taking oaths (swearing) in courts of law?
6. What is the significance of Frederick Tolles's observation that Friends historically can be divided between the "absolutists" and the "relativists"?

CHAPTER *9*

Last Things
and Eternal Hope

Having dealt with the essential elements of Quaker faith, belief, and practice, the question naturally arises: What is the point of all this? What is the ultimate end or purpose of life and history on this planet? And what comes after this? Is there any meaningful terminal point or goal toward which nature and history are moving? All of which leads us to the final consideration in any doctrinal or theological study: eschatology.

Put simply, eschatology is a study of "last things" in relationship to what we call "the eternal hope." In biblical and Christian history a number of terms have been used to describe the end of time as we know it—among them, "the Day of the Lord" and "the Last Judgment." These imply not only a goal or purpose, but also human accountability; and it is this sense of moral and spiritual accountability that gives purpose and meaning to eschatology.

There are various dimensions to this branch of theology that may be concerned with final events in the history of the world and humanity: for example, what does eschatology mean in terms of the movement of nature and history; does our concern for eschatology extend beyond the realm of our knowledge and experience (that is, beyond history) to include the cosmos itself; and how does our own person (our own individual consciousness and awareness) fit into the scheme of things? Does our own being, our selfhood, have ultimate meaning and significance, or are we in the final analysis inchoate and inert matter? Again, put quite simply, we want to know the answers to two questions: What is the meaning and purpose of life for us collectively, and what is the meaning and purpose of life for us personally?

These questions are not easily answered; perhaps they cannot be answered at all—at least to the satisfaction of the rational mind. But the quest for meaning in life drives us to seek the best answers we can find. Certainly Quakers seek answers as much as anyone else, which brings us to the Quaker perspective on eschatology.

The Early Quaker View

Seventeenth–century Friends had a much clearer awareness and understanding of last things than we do today. Partly this can be attributed to the fact that in those days it was a tradition within Christendom to deal seriously with such matters. Recent generations have been the product of the nineteenth century view of evolutionary development and the progress theory of history that believed everything was getting better and better all the time. Our present generation, however, harbors a new preoccupation with end time because of the frightful nuclear age in which we live. Also, two world wars, the Holocaust in Nazi Germany, and many other world-shaking events have brought us to a point where we not only deny that there is any such thing as steady and predictable progress in history, but we have even begun to question human survival itself. In this sense we have something in common with those seventeenth–century Quakers, or even the early

Christians in New Testament times.

George Fox had a well-defined philosophy of history, based on his biblical understanding.[1] He believed that there were three stages or ages of history. The first preceded Adam's fall, when the image of God was fully manifest in human life. The second stage began with Adam's fall, when people had to be governed by outward laws and restraints. And the third stage, Fox believed, was marked by the coming of Christ (the Messiah), beginning a new age in which fallen human beings could be restored to a state of reconciliation with God. It was this last age into which Fox called people, a state of obedience to Christ that called one to live *as if* the kingdom had already arrived.

It is significant that Fox and early Friends were dependent upon the book of Revelation for their understanding of the end times and used much of the language found there to describe their eschatology. It has become commonplace among liberal Friends to point out their indebtedness to the Johannine writings in the New Testament, especially with reference to the doctrine of the Light. Evangelical Friends, on the other hand, draw more heavily from the Pauline writings of the New Testament. Both traditions have tended to overlook Fox's indebtedness to the language and thought of the book of Revelation. In recent years Douglas Gwyn has studied early Quaker eschatology with these facts in mind,[2] and he says that "Revelation forms the centerpiece of his [Fox's] apocalyptic message."[3] Fox also made much use of the apocalyptic language of Revelation to express the struggles he experienced between the forces of good and evil.

The apocalyptic language in Revelation is symbolic and assumes a dualism between the forces of good and evil resident in persons, the world, and the cosmos. James Nayler, an early Quaker, described this struggle as the "Lamb's War," which takes its cue from biblical sources by claiming that Christ, the Lamb of God, would finally be victorious over Satan. Fox and other early Friends also used the same imagery.

Fox used the language of Revelation to detail his interpretation of history. For example, the whore of Babylon (Rev. 17-19) symbolized alienation from God caused by the Antichrist. The dragon (Rev. 12:9) represented Satan. The beast (Rev. 13) continued the dragon image of evil, and Fox linked this with the false church of persecution, swearing, oaths, titles, and false teaching. The woman (Rev. 12) was the image of the true church, which had been forced into the wilderness by Satan, thus marking the apostasy of the church from the time of Christ to the seventeenth century. Gwyn believes that Fox's view was distinguished by his focus on the church as apostate, rather than on the political order or the state, which is the interpretation often given. Thus, claims Gwyn, Fox was primarily concerned with the fall of the church rather than with the demise of the political order.[4]

Fox believed the Lamb (Rev. 17:14) would overcome the Antichrist, a victory that would be marked in history by "the Day of the Lord." But early Friends also believed that the corporate body of faithful Christians could experience the Lamb's victory in such a way as to produce what was referred to as "the Camp of the Lord." For Fox this marked the gathering of the people of God into the kingdom. He believed that everyone would experience this "day of visitation," the means of salvation for all people if they would repent and accept the way of obedience and righteousness. Thus "the Day of the Lord" is a day of judgment as well as a day of victory over sin and evil, whether it be personal or corporate in scope.

In preparation for the Day of the Lord Fox felt called to preach that "Christ has come to teach his people himself." This was an apocalyptic message because it was the Quaker equivalent of the Second Coming of Christ and a sign that the last days were at hand. It was the Quaker way of saying that Christ has already come and one need not wait for a future coming in order to enter the kingdom. The call of God is *now*, not at some future time. In Fox's day this was a radical message, and if adhered to it continues to be a radical message today.

Fox believed in the Arminian doctrine of free will, allowing for the possibility that, although God intends the salvation of all, some may not respond in obedience. In his study of Fox's view of last things, Canby Jones says that Fox did not have hope for the unrepentant and wicked; they were subject to eternal punishment.[5] In this sense he was not a universalist in salvation doctrine, even though the potential for universal acceptance was always there. Fox did, however, object to the Calvinist doctrine of double predestination (election and reprobation)—that is, the belief that some are elected to salvation and others to damnation. For Fox, only those who continued in disobedience to the saving Light of Christ were subject to condemnation.

Friends did not dwell much on the traditional concepts of heaven and hell. They accepted them in principle, as with many other doctrines, but their emphasis was on a present rather than a futuristic understanding of them. Heaven and hell held personal and experiential meaning rather than being "places" of reward and punishment, though they did not deny the latter.

The question remains, however, whether Friends today believe in universal salvation. Do they believe that all persons and all creation will finally become reconciled with God, the Creator? Certainly Friends believe in this possibility and hope. Early Friends referred to every person's "day of visitation" and believed that if one did not respond faithfully at these times he or she ran the risk of never having another opportunity to become reconciled with God; yet they were never altogether clear on what the consequences were if one did not respond. Given Friends emphasis on the goodness and love of God, it seems inconceivable that such a God would allow any to perish, even if that requires that God act as the Hound of Heaven to pursue one unto death and beyond. Apart from this expression of faith and hope we can say nothing more.

Like the Calvinist (Puritan) tradition Friends emphasized the three-fold offices of Christ—prophet, priest, and king—thus setting forth a functional view of Christology. [6] The big difference between Friends and their Puritan forebears was that Friends focused on the prophetic and kingly roles of Christ rather than the priestly role. Because the Puritans emphasized the latter they seemed always to be looking backward to the atonement of Christ and what it did to assure salvation. Although Friends acknowledged the atoning work of Christ, they had an eschatological orientation, looking forward to Christ leading them into the kingdom of God—to the new age under the new covenant of God's righteousness.

The final question is whether Fox and the early Friends sought a purely spiritual kingdom, or whether they believed that the physical world and the social order could also be transformed. In Quaker history there have been two readings of this. The traditional view declares that God works through institutions and structures of both church and state to accomplish the divine will for humankind and society (see chapter 10). This is essentially a one-kingdom (as opposed to a two-kingdom) view of the world, based on a single ethical standard; and it requires that an exacting ethic be applied to social and political history in order to bring the world into harmony with the will of God.

The other view, for which there is some evidence in the writings of Fox and early Friends, sounds like the Anabaptist position. It emphasizes the Gospel Order rather than the political and social order and holds that this order is to be realized through God's holy order—namely, the church rather than the state. This position still insists on a single ethical standard, the ethic of Christ (as reflected in the Sermon on the Mount), but early Friends also struck a prophetic note by claiming that the kingdoms of this world are to be transformed and made over into the kingdom of righteousness. This being so, the kingdoms of this world remain in outer darkness until they come under the Gospel of Christ and his true church. [7]

The Gospel of Eternal Hope

Although Friends today seldom express themselves in the apocalyptic language of the book of Revelation, they do recognize that we live in perilous times which call for dramatic responses. Yet Friends continue to proclaim a gospel of hope based on their belief in the power and love of God to overcome the sin and evil that prevail in our world. When it is based on a too-simplistic optimism or false idealism, this hope turns out to be deceptive and flawed and fails to take the depth of sin and evil seriously enough. But Quakerism at its best is rooted in a faith that, in spite of the dark side of life, God's power and love are great enough to redeem the demonic forces of life. Today, as in the seventeenth century, Friends need to ground their confidence in a theology of hope, as articulated by George Fox in his well-known passage about the Light that can dispel the darkness:

And the Lord answered that it was needful I should speak to all conditions; and in this I saw the infinite love of God. I saw also that there was an ocean of darkness and death, but an infinite ocean of light and love, which flowed over the ocean of darkness. And in that also I saw the infinite love of God; and I had great openings. [8]

This conviction that there is an ocean of light and love that can overcome the ocean of darkness and death is the basis for Fox's theology of hope. He understood that this applied not only to one's personal life, but to the world as well. Fox envisioned "a great people to be gathered." This was the good news of the Gospel that Fox proclaimed to the people of his day, and it continues to form the basis for a gospel of hope for us today. And the source of such hope is not humanity's natural capacity for goodness, but our belief in the power and grace of God to overcome sin and evil in such a way as to enable believers by the Light of Christ to "be doers of the word, and not hearers only" (James 1:22). Fox saw this taking place in the community of faith (the church) where the power of God restrains evil and allows communal accountability and responsibility.

This doctrine of the Light that overcomes the darkness also reflects the perfectionist ethic of early Quakers (see chapter 5), which always insisted on "real righteousness" rather than "surrogate righteousness" imputed by Christ. One must never be justified *in* one's sin but be sanctified (or redeemed) *from* sin. Moreover, early Friends refused to settle for a futuristic coming of the kingdom in place of the possibility of a realized reconciliation here and now. Such claims would be presumptuous except for their reliance upon the grace and power of God to fulfill these promises. What this calls for, however, is a new and majestic understanding of God that is vastly greater than the truncated "that of God in every one" theology of many Friends.

Hope for Life After Death

So we come to the eschatological question everyone finally asks: "What is the meaning of my life in this vast universe? Does it have any ultimate significance beyond the space and time world in which I live now?" Or, more simply put, "Is there life after death?"

If considered in too narrow a context this becomes a very self-centered, self-serving concern. But seen in its larger setting, it affirms the human sense of accountability and responsibility to the Source of our being, which is central to what it means to have been created in the image of God. Benedict, considered "the Patriarch of Western Monasticism," counseled his monks: "Keep your own death before your eyes each day." Commenting on this, Parker Palmer has said: "This is not a counsel of morbidity but a reminder to keep looking for signs of larger life."[9] It is this larger life about which we have not only a right but an obligation to be concerned.

Traditionally the question of life after death has been referred to as the doctrine of immortality and has to do with the extent and the way in which human selfhood endures beyond earthly existence. It is important here to distinguish between the Platonic view of immortality and the biblical view because most doctrines of immortality are dependent on one or the other.

The Platonic view considers the soul indestructible and eternal. It comes from God (the Divine) and is implanted in a physical body during the life of the individual person. At death the soul returns to the Source of its being. Thus it endures through all the vicissitudes of life and death.

In contrast to this, the New Testament view is that the individual self (or soul) is created by God, and when physical life terminates, the whole self (body, mind, and spirit) passes through a real death. Once the self dies, it can be raised again in the resurrection by the re-creative power of God. There is no indestructible soul, as such, that endures; but there is an enduring Source, God the Creator, who gives life and being to each person. Insofar as there is life after death, it is life re-created and sustained by God. Apart from God there is no hope because there is no creative and sustaining source of life. The paradigm for this understanding of life after death is, of course, the death and resurrection of Jesus. Jesus does not continue to live because he possessed an indestructible soul, but because of the power of God to raise up a new life (1 Cor. 15).

Quakers have never bothered to develop a very sophisticated view of life after death, but historically they clearly have emphasized the power of God to transform and sustain life in new dimensions. They have always sought the living presence of God as the foremost spiritual reality, and no speculation or doctrine would suffice as a substitute. Indeed their strong emphasis on the Holy Spirit stems from the Christian experience of the resurrected Christ: the promise that Jesus would send another Counselor, Comforter, or Advocate in his place (John 14:25-26). This liberation of the Christ Within has always been the source of new life and hope for Friends.

To claim that all or most Quakers subscribe to this biblical view of life after death would be an overstatement, however. There are Friends who believe, in the Platonic sense, that by virtue of our existence we have an immortal spiritual connectedness with the source of our being, whether they call it "that of God in every one," the Divine center, or whatever. Others build a case for immortality on psychological grounds—namely, the continuity of conscious personality. Another view places primary emphasis on eternity as a qualitative vs quantitative view of life after death. The claim is that human beings who are grounded in historical time have the capacity to participate in God's time; or to put it another way, they are able to participate in the beyond in the here-and-now. Finally, there are those who make no claim at all about life after death, but simply believe that life as we know it ceases to exist at the point of death and that we pass into oblivion in a state of nothingness.

Facing the Final Frontier

One of the characteristics of Quakers is that we choose not to speculate too much about death and dying. Instead, we focus on whether we are living, at this very moment, in the presence and power of God so that we will be sustained in whatever death brings. As Fox would say, we live "in the virtue of that life and power," which will enable us to conduct ourselves as if the kingdom were already present.

Such a stance also suggests that we must live in an attitude of prayer. E. Herman's classic work, *Creative Prayer*, teaches that prayer is basically surrendering ourselves to God.[10] It is a pilgrimage of movement from a self-centered life to a God-centered life. Herman says that prayer is humbly lifting ourselves up to God in a desire to know God and be made one with God. A similar attitude is captured by Charles Whiston's suggestion for a daily prayer:

> O Lord Christ, in obedience to Thy claim upon me, I surrender myself to Thee this day; all that I am and all that I have belong wholly and unconditionally to thee for thy using. Take me away from myself, and use me up as Thou wilt, when Thou wilt, where Thou wilt, and with whom Thou wilt. [11]

Even though the accounts of Gethsemane and the passion of Jesus clearly teach us that we all have to go through the eye of the needle of death, the anguish and agony can be made victorious if we are living in the life and power of God. Like Jesus, we may feel forsaken in the hour of death and cry out as he did, but there are also assurances that our cries will not go unheard nor will we be deserted at such times:

> The Lord is my shepherd, I shall not want.... Even though I walk through the valley of the shadow of death, I fear no evil; for thou art with me; thy rod and thy staff, they comfort me (Psalm 23:1-4).

James Nayler, the seventeenth century Quaker martyr, expressed the same spirit when he was beaten and left to die:

There is a Spirit which I feel that delights to do no evil, nor to revenge any wrong, but delights to endure all things, in hope to enjoy its own in the end... I found it alone, being forsaken. I have fellowship therein with them who live in dens and desolate places in the earth, who through death obtained this resurrection and eternal holy life.[12]

And perhaps the best conclusion to our final battle in this life is found in the prayer of the Apostle Paul in 1 Corinthians 15:54-55. Whether or not we fully understand Paul's words, they certainly speak powerfully to the matter of death and the promise of resurrection:

> Death is swallowed up in victory.
> O death, where is thy victory?
> O death, where is thy sting?
> The sting of death is sin, and the power of sin is the law.
> But thanks be to God, who gives us the victory through our Lord Jesus Christ.

Questions for Discussion

1. What is the meaning of "eschatology"? How does it affect our lives?
2. Can there be any moral order in the universe without a sense of ultimate accountability to God?
3. What was the significance of "the Day of the Lord" and "the day of visitation" for early Friends?
4. What is the relationship between George Fox's proclamation, "Christ has come to teach his people himself," and the biblical idea of the second coming of Christ?
5. What is the basis for a Quaker theology of hope?
6. What is the distinction between the Platonic view of the immortality of the soul and the biblical concept of the resurrection of the body and life after death?

CHAPTER 10

Quaker, Mission, Service and Outreach

I n the previous chapters we have discussed what Quakers believe, including Chapter 8, "The Quaker Testimonies," which deal with the roots and motivation for Quaker missions and service. Now let us look at some of the ways that Quaker faith and practice have been brought together in mission, service, and outreach.

Although Friends place a premium on practicing what they believe, and although they are known for many good works in the world, they are often perceived as reluctant to propagate their faith for the purpose of gaining new members. However, the moods and practices of Friends in this respect have varied. Early Friends were both zealous and aggressive in proclaiming their message to the world. They seemed to have an apocalyptic sense of end time and, like their New Testament forebears, felt called to reach as many people as possible with the Gospel message; yet they seemed relatively unconcerned about establishing new settlements or meetings that would become identified with the Friends movement.

As we have discussed, there was a middle period of Quakerism when Friends withdrew unto themselves, followed by the nineteenth-century missionary outreach patterned somewhat after the prevailing mission-ary thrust of other churches. In more recent times many Friends have preferred to share their faith by service to others rather than by proclaiming it in word for the purpose of winning others to the Christian way. But even here, there are important exceptions. Evangeli-cal Quakers today place great emphasis on evangelistic outreach and church growth, while at the other extreme there are Friends who seem to think that Quakerism is a secret to be guarded.

In spite of these differences, throughout their history Friends have felt the persistent impulse to make their faith relevant to real life and to try to lead others, either by word, deed, or example, to this treasured life of the kingdom. As mentioned in connection with the testimonies, there is the strong hope and belief that life, both personal and social, can be made over and improved, if not perfected. Seth Hinshaw, formerly Superintendent of North Carolina Yearly Meeting (FUM), expressed the general mood and outlook of early Friends when he said: "Early Quakers were persons whose lives had been electrified by the power of the living Christ and who felt called and commissioned to go forth and change the world."[1] And although not all Friends have experienced this clarion call through the years, it has remained a cherished hope in their lives. Moreover, they have been for the most part a compassionate people so that a ministry of service and reconciliation to those in need has marked the Quaker movement from the beginning.

In order to examine how Friends have witnessed to their faith, we shall turn to a brief summary of their record in several important categories of outreach into the world: philanthropy; political activity; business and commerce; missionary outreach; relief service; and educa-tion. As we undertake this survey, keep in mind that Friends began as an agricultural and working-class people. In the course of their history they moved from agriculture to business, commerce, and the professions until eventually they became mostly middle–class and well–educated. This shift in economic and social status has had much to do with the way Friends have come to live out their faith in the world.

Philanthropy

The circumstances that Friends found themselves in during the second half of the seventeenth century furnished the agenda for some of their concerns. Naturally they were eager to gain greater religious freedom and to influence the government and courts in ways that would guarantee such freedom. Within a generation this led them to America. But in the midst of this they still had to deal with the suffering they encountered in their imprisonments and in miscarriages of justice, which seemed to develop in them a special concern for the conditions of the prisons and a desire to work for justice before the law.

Friends, such as John Bellers (1654-1725), were responsive to the conditions of poverty among victims of the factory system in England, resulting from the Industrial Revolution. The general economic climate was one of depressed wages and an unfair land enclosure system that favored the wealthy and hurt the poor. At the end of the seventeenth century Bellers experimented with what he called "colleges of industry" made up of colonies of three hundred persons in agricultural and fishing trades and designed to provide a livelihood for these impoverished people.

The eighteenth century marked the beginning of Quaker anti-slavery work championed by John Woolman (1720-1772), Anthony Benezet (1713-1784), and others. It was also marked by Friends' concern for the humane treatment of the American Indians, whose cause William Penn had championed when he first settled the Pennsylvania colony in 1681. The nineteenth century also saw the beginning of the Lancasterian School System, promoted by Joseph Lancaster (1778-1836), which provided a low-cost popular education where older students instructed younger ones. And Quaker concern for the insane became evident by the establishment of Pennsylvania Hospital in 1757, York Retreat in England in 1796, and the Frankford Asylum in Philadelphia in 1813.

At the turn of the nineteenth century the plight of laboring people, exemplified by the poverty and suffering of the silk weavers in Spitalfields in London's East End, claimed the attention of some well-known Quaker philanthropists, including scientist and statesman William Allen (1770-1844), Peter Bedford (1780-1864), and William Forster (1784-1854). They established the Spitalfields soup kitchens and set up industrial schools away from the cities to retrain the impoverished workers. The early part of the century also saw the remarkable prison reform work at Newgate Prison in London by Elizabeth Gurney Fry (1780-1845). Although Friends had been concerned about prison conditions at the beginning of the Society, this marked an expanding involvement in prison work.

Quaker abolitionist reformers intensified in the nineteenth century. William Forster, along with non-Quakers such as William Wilberforce and Thomas Buxton, worked toward the freeing of England's slaves in 1833. Later Joseph John Gurney worked to have Engand free its colonial slaves. In America many Quaker names became associated with the anti-slavery movement. Among the most prominent were Elias Hicks (1748-1830), Levi Coffin (1798-1877), Lucretia Mott (1793-1880), and John Greenleaf Whittier (1807-1892). Levi Coffin became known for his work with the Underground Railroad, which helped many slaves escape to freedom. Lucretia Mott not only engaged in anti-slavery work but was prominent in the beginnings of the feminist movement in America. And of course Whittier became known both for his work to free slaves as well as his poetry, becoming the best-known Quaker poet of the nineteenth century. Following the Civil War Friends were in the forefront of the Freedmen Societies' work to rehabilitate ex-slaves.

Other philanthropic concerns claiming the energies of Friends included temperance work, opposition to capital punishment, women's rights and suffrage, and the establishment of Peace Societies in the nineteenth century.

Political Activity

Politics is the art of governing, which in turn is one of the major ways in which history is shaped. In the beginning Quakers shared the Puritan (Calvinist) view that because God is the final molder of history, the political shaping of history is one of the ways God works in the world. It was believed that through this process Friends were called to become co-workers with God. Thus Friends, although not generally known as astute politicians, have not shied away from helping to shape the course of history through political education and action.

The actual involvement of Quakers in political life has been greater than one might expect from a group that has consistently taken a position of conscientious objection to war and other social evils—a group in England that was prevented from holding public office until 1832 because they refused to take the oath of office. However, after the British Reform Act of 1832, which permitted Friends to take the affirmation in place of the oath of office, a steady flow of Quakers entered Parliament. Fifty-two English Friends held seats in this body between 1833-1937. Joseph Pease (1799-1872) was the first Friend to be elected to Parliament, serving from 1833-1841. Joseph Sturge (1793-1860) stood for Parliament twice and was defeated, but still led an active public life. Best known, of course, was John Bright (1811-1889), who was not only a distinguished member of Parliament but served in the prime minister's cabinet under Gladstone.

Many Quakers also stood for elective office at the local level. By 1916 there were as many as 110 Quaker justices of the peace, and in the 1940s it was estimated that approximately 1,000 Friends were serving in government at some level. In 1900 London Yearly Meeting stated that public service was a duty for Friends, and the Quaker periodicals reflected much the same view. In recent years, however, the trend has been away from public office with greater emphasis on involvement in public life and service through a variety of social service and humanitarian channels.[2]

On the other side of the Atlantic the story has been quite different. When Friends arrived in America they immediately began to assert themselves in public life and exerted strong political influence, except in places where they were barred, such as Massachusetts and Virginia. In Rhode Island they had a large share in the control of the government for over a hundred years, from 1663-1774; during this period thirty-six terms of the governorship were held by Quakers. In North Carolina, which was largely a Quaker colony at the beginning, John Archdale was a distinguished governor (1695-1699) who brought about many reforms and improvements. For a time Friends also controlled West Jersey, attempting to implement some of the principles of government that were more fully instituted in Pennsylvania. In 1682, Quaker apologist Robert Barclay was appointed governor *in absentia* of East Jersey. When East and West Jersey were combined to form New Jersey in 1702, Quaker influence began to decline.

By far the most extensive Quaker attempt at government, of course, was the Pennsylvania "Holy Experiment" of William Penn, which was chartered by Charles II in 1681. Penn's primary aim was to establish a colony where religious liberty could be enjoyed. At the same time the Frame of Government incorporated the principles of civil liberty, popular government, and the right of a fair trial by jury. Penn spent little time in the colony himself but governed through his personal representatives, William Markham and James Logan. After a difficult beginning the colony enjoyed approximately thirty good years. Then about 1740 difficulties arose that culminated in a crisis over the assembly's non-support of the Crown's involvement in the French and Indian War. This finally was cause for the Quaker majority to withdraw from the Assembly in 1756; thereafter the longstanding influence of Friends in the Pennsylvania government declined, never to be restored.

After their withdrawal from the Pennsylvania government, almost immediately Friends expressed caution about further involvement in political life. In writing about this new attitude and its long-term consequences, Frederick Tolles said:

> In 1758, two years after the Quaker abdication in Pennsylvania, Philadelphia Yearly Meeting advised its members to "beware of accepting of, or continuing in, the exercise of any office or station in civil society or government" which required actions inconsistent with Quaker testimonies. The pendulum had swung sharply away from political activity, and I think it is fair to say that American Friends have tended almost from that day to this to avoid direct participation in politics, at least in the sense of seeking elective office. [3]

Although this attitude toward public service became the prevailing point of view for well over a century, eventually some Friends did venture into the political arena.[4] Several have served in both the U.S. Senate and the House of Representatives, including Senator Paul

Douglas from Chicago; several governorships have been held by Friends; and two members of Friends, Herbert Hoover and Richard Nixon, have held the U.S. Presidency. In England Quakers have continued in politics in a limited way, perhaps the most notable in the nineteenth century being Member of Parliament T. Edmund Harvey (1875-1955).

The most common political involvement of Friends, however, has been their long-term attempt to influence public policy by visiting public officials or addressing them in other ways. Tolles says this has been a practice of Friends from the beginning and cites the efforts of the Meeting for Sufferings of London Yearly Meeting to coordinate lobbying work in the beginning years of the Society of Friends:

> The weightiest Friends in England, including George Fox and William Penn, busied themselves buttonholing Members of Parliament and appearing at committee hearings. The Yearly Meeting even rented a room in a coffeehouse hard by the Houses of Parliament for a headquarters . . . . The legislative struggle for religious liberty was substantially won in 1689 with the passage of the great Toleration Act, but the lobbying efforts went on, until Friends were finally granted the right to substitute a simple affirmation for a formal oath in 1722. From time to time in the course of this campaign the Meeting for Sufferings urged Friends to write their Parliament men on the subject. If anyone thinks the techniques of the Friends Committee on National Legislation, the Quaker lobby in Washington, are a modern innovation, he knows little of Quaker history.[5]

Tolles again points out that this method of influencing government has not only been practiced by Friends historically, but he suggests that it is the most appropriate way for Quakers to shape the laws and policies of their governments:

> I should like to suggest . . . that if there is any distinctive Quaker posture *vis a vis* politics, it is . . . the prophetic stance or role of the divine lobbyist. By this I do not mean approaching legislators for favors—though Friends have sometimes done that, as in the case of the Affirmation Act [of 1722]. I am thinking rather of George Fox in 1656 bidding Oliver Cromwell to lay down his crown at the feet of Jesus, of Robert Barclay in 1679 standing before the representative of the European powers at Nimwegen and calling upon them to settle a peace upon Christian principles, or Joseph Sturge in 1855 pleading with Tsar Alexander II for reconciliation with England, of Rufus Jones in 1938 interceding for the Jews before the chiefs of the Gestapo, or any Friend visiting his congressman with a religious concern. All these, like the prophets of Israel, have felt a divine call to "speak Truth to power," to lay a concern upon those who are charged with the governing of men. The Friends Committee on National Legislation [in Washington] is, in a sense, an institutionalization of this age-old Quaker practice. [6]

Thus Friends have had a long and important involvement with government, both inside and out. Their track record for holding public office has not been notable, but their faithfulness to the inward requirements of conscience has had its impact in many ways. For this they have become known and, for the most part, respected for the witness they have made in the causes of peace, justice, and human freedom.

Business and Commerce

Although their involvement in either politics or business has never been officially under the care of the Meeting, Friends have exercised testimonies that have attempted to admonish and sometimes restrain their members in carrying out such endeavors. Embodied in Queries and Advices, these testimonies have provided Friends with practical guidance about business and professional matters. Since Friends believe their vocational life should be rooted in their religious life, it is important to see how their religious convictions are expressed in public life and in the workplace, for it is in these areas that Quaker faith and practice do not always coincide. However, Friends concern for integrity has been manifested in the business world and in the professions. For example, reference was made to the Friends testimony of a one price system in merchandizing, which reflected their commitment to integrity both in pricing and in the quality of goods and services offered for sale.

We have already noted that at the beginning Friends were primarily agricultural and working–class people; but in the latter part of the eighteenth and into the nineteenth centuries, along with the rest of society, many moved into business, commerce, industry, and science. As they did so, they became increasingly middle class economically and socially and sometimes moved into circles of society at a higher level than that. So while we need to keep in mind that a substantial number of Friends today remain farmers, housewives, school teachers, social workers, factory employees, and manual laborers, the broad influence of Friends in business, industry, and commerce is impressive.[7]

First to become known in commerce were the English Quakers who were prominent in the banking business, such as the Gurneys, Barclays, and Lloyds. The latter two names are still associated with banks all over the world, although they now have little, if any, Quaker connection. The

Gurneys also engaged in woolen manufacturing and weaving in Norwich, England. Another group of Quaker families, the Cadburys, Frys, and Rowntrees, were makers of cocoa and chocolate, an industry begun in large measure to counter the problem of intemperance. In place of alcoholic drinks these imaginative Friends provided the substitute of cocoa. Several business mergers have since taken place, so for the most part the identity with the Quaker family names has been lost in these companies.

The Pease family, especially Edward Pease, was associated with the railway industry in England. But perhaps the most interesting of all was Abraham Darby from Coalbrookdale, England, who discovered a method for smelting iron from coke which was essential to manufacturing a good grade of steel. Concerning the influence of this man Kenneth Boulding has observed:

In terms of sheer quantity of influence it may well be that Abraham Darby of Coalbrookdale, was the most influential Quaker in three centuries. Part of the wilderness into which John Woolman traveled to Wyalusing [to visit the Indians] is now occupied by the Bethlehem Steel Works which would hardly have been possible without Abraham Darby's discovery of the method of smelting coke. The economic base for the great upsurge of English-speaking people in the last two hundred years owes a great deal to the hard work and ingenuity of the eighteenth-century Quakers in advancing science and industry.[8]

The extent to which Quaker testimonies have affected Friends in the workplace and in public service is difficult to assess. There is evidence, however, that the testimonies of integrity, peace, and justice have had marked influence. Though they have never transformed the world into the "Peaceable Kingdom," which has been the vision of many Friends, still a difference has been made and Friends have come to be known the world over for their humanitarian service and their vision for world peace.

Quaker Missions

A strong missionary spirit caused early Friends to proclaim the Gospel message and call people to repentance. Friends became known as "Publishers of Truth," and in the 1660s, with their headquarters at Swarthmoor Hall in Northwest England, they formed a close-knit group of itinerant ministers who were known as the "valiant sixty." Swarthmoor Hall was the home of Margaret Fell who married George Fox in 1669 and has been called the "Mother of Quakerism." Through the Kendal Fund, which she administered, support money was provided for Friends in prison and for the traveling ministry. The "valiant sixty" was a movement of men and women in their late teens and twenties who went first to London, Bristol, and Norwich to proclaim the Gospel message. Later they traveled to Europe and to the American colonies to carry the message abroad.

Hugh Barbour describes this missionary thrust with the language of James Nayler (from the mid-1650s) as a "conquest of evil" in the "Lamb's war."[9] The objective was the transformation of all life, personal and social. It was an ambitious program that Friends set before themselves, but they lived under the sense of "end time," as did the early New Testament Christians, which accounted for their sense of urgency about their mission. George Fox urged not only his own followers but other Christians as well to "go among the Turks, Tartars, Blacks and Indians and give unto them freely as Christ gave himself freely."[10] By the end of the century, Neave Brayshaw points out, these itinerant Quaker ministers had little to show for their efforts. He thinks they may have overestimated the responsiveness of their hearers, and probably because of their apocalyptic sense of "end-time" they did not see the need for "sustained educational and pastoral work."[11]

Although the itinerant ministry continued among Friends throughout the eighteenth century, during the period of quietistic withdrawal it was primarily a ministry of visitation among Friends rather than outreach to people beyond the Society. Friends expended great energy and time shoring up their own organizational and institutional needs, and not without reason. The early fire had gone out of the Quaker ministry. Friends were not being jailed as they had been in the early years, so they were no longer driven by this kind of persecution. Although the eighteenth century was not quite the historical low point some have made it out to be, since Quakers were still involved in public service and philanthropy, it was not until the nineteenth century that Friends began to sense a new call to missionary service. Part of this awakening resulted from the influence of evangelical Christianity on Quakerism, both in England and America, along with an awareness of the expanding colonial world of the British Empire and the sense of need resulting from Western imperialism in these faraway places.

Concern for missionary outreach was first voiced at London Yearly Meeting in the early 1830s, but it was many years before such activity was officially endorsed. The quietistic fear of "creaturely activity" and their disapproval of the "paid ministry" kept Friends from engaging in missionary work in any organized way. At the same time they did endorse and support philanthropic work, entailing "paid work" in the name of the Society. It must also be remembered that after the 1832 Reform Act in England Friends emerged in many new ways, including standing for public office. The Quaker "coming out" in the nineteenth century was marked by new signs of outreach in both mission and service, and a brief listing of some Friends who were involved in these new fields of ministry and service will begin to tell the story:

1823—Hannah Kilham went to Sierra Leone;

1830—James Backhouse went to Australia;

1833—Daniel Wheeler went to the South Sea Islands;

1846—Isaac Sharp went to Iceland, Greenland, and Labrador;

1846-47—William Forster undertook relief work among victims of the Irish potato famine;

1857—Eli and Sybil Jones went to Liberia, and in 1867 to Palestine;

1858—George Richardson, at age seventy-eight, began work in Norway;

1866—Rachel Metcalfe went to India;

1867—Joseph Sewell went to Madagascar and was joined by Louis and Sarah Street from the U.S.

One could continue to list missionary thrusts by individuals, but 1860 is sometimes cited as the beginning of Friends' organized missionary work. The earlier missionaries, such as James Backhouse and Daniel Wheeler, did not go with the intention of establishing organized missions or settlements. They still followed in the tradition of the itinerant minister, concerned to carry a message to certain individuals or groups of people. In 1860 in a letter to *The Friend* George Richardson, who had a missionary vision for Friends, observed that "brief and transient visits, though very useful for instruction and edification, are not all that is required for the conversion of heathen nations."[12] So from 1860 on we begin to see organized missions as compared with the personal evangelism prior to that time.

In 1868 the nucleus of the Foreign Missionary Society was formed in England. For many years it carried on significant missionary work, but it was not officially recognized by London Yearly Meeting until 1917. By 1920 it was estimated that British Friends had 120 missionaries in active work in Bhopal, India, Ceylon, Pemba, Syria, and Madagascar.[13]

In America, Friends organized missionary work in similar fashion. Indiana Yearly Meeting established a Foreign Missionary Society in 1870, while other yearly meetings developed comparable missionary efforts. Stanley Pumphrey, an English Friend, visited America from 1875-1879 and encouraged Friends to engage in missionary work, including the formation of a central mission board. The Quinquennial Friends Conferences, which began in Richmond, Indiana, in 1887 and culminated in the formation of the Five Years Meeting of Friends (now Friends United Meeting) in 1902, exhibited a strong concern for missions.

In 1894 the American Friends Board of Foreign Missions was independently organized at Wilmington, Ohio. It originally had no administrative function, but soon assumed oversight of newly formed missionary work in Cuba. When Five Years Meeting was organized in 1902 it soon incorporated the American Friends Board of Missions, which in turn took responsibility for all American missionary efforts except those of Canada, Philadelphia, and Ohio (Damascus). From 1907-1912 Charles E. Tebbetts served as the administrative head of the mission board and began to implement the missionary recommendations that came out of the ecumenical Edinburgh Missionary Conference of 1910.[14]

In 1902 the Friends Africa Industrial Mission began work in British East Africa (now Kenya) under the leadership of three American Friends: Arthur C. Chilson, Edgar T. Hole, and Willis Hotchkiss. In 1964, East Africa Yearly Meeting was given control over the property and projects of the East Africa Mission, and in due course E.A.Y.M.

became the largest Friends mission in the world. Only recently has it been divided into multiple yearly meeting groups.

In subsequent years California Yearly Meeting undertook missionary work in Guatemala, Honduras, and Alaska; Oregon Yearly Meeting in Alaska, Bolivia, and Peru; and Kansas Yearly Meeting in Burundi (East Africa). Ohio (Damascus) Yearly Meeting developed work in India, China, and Taiwan; and Philadelphia Yearly Meeting, together with Baltimore and Canadian Yearly Meetings, took up work in Japan. New England Yearly Meeting had work in Syria; New York, Indiana, and Western Yearly Meetings developed work in Mexico; and Iowa Yearly Meeting assumed responsibility for work in Jamaica.

Friends have also carried on extensive mission, service, and educational work among the American Indians, chiefly under the Associated Executive Committee of Friends for Indian Affairs, established by Orthodox Friends in 1869. We cannot here do justice to the extensive involvement of Friends in Indian work from the time of William Penn's first encounter with them down to the present day. Suffice it to say that even today Friends carry out legislative action on their behalf in Washington and provide goods and services to the Indians in the field.

Although Friends missions may not be as active and aggressive as they were a generation ago, efforts are still made to find new areas of service. A good example is the Chicago Fellowship of Friends. This is an inner–city ministry undertaken by Steve and Marlene Pedigo, and sponsored by Friends United Meeting. Another development in a Third World country has been the work of Sadie Vernon in Belize in Central America. Also there have been efforts by Johan Maurer during his tenure as general secretary of FUM to encourage the formation of Quaker groups in Russia, and similar formations in Lithuania by Violete Tribandiene, a native of the country educated in America.

While it is true that some Quaker missionaries have had "winning souls for Christ" as their priority, Friends generally have been noted for a holistic approach to mission work. This broader emphasis addresses the needs of the whole person as well as the surrounding culture. Hence, building schools for education, hospitals for health care, and industrial and agricultural training for practical economic help have been priorities. In recent years it has also been a policy to turn the mission work and property assets over to the indigenous people as quickly as possible so they do not continue to be dependent upon foreign missionaries. But underlying the entire enterprise is Friends' concern for the spiritual needs and welfare of the people, an emphasis that provides continuity with that first missionary outreach when itinerant ministers went forth from Swarthmoor Hall to carry the Gospel message. Friends believe the Gospel is both personal and social and therefore must be concerned with the whole person and the whole world.

Quaker Service

There is a widespread view that the purpose of missions is to win people to the Christian way of life, whereas service meets human needs without reference to any personal commitment of faith. Thus Quaker outreach in the form of missions has usually been in the name of Christ, whereas Quaker service has been in the name of Friends, but not for the purpose of proselytizing. We must be careful about making such generalizations, however, since much work in the name of missions has a service quality to it, such as the industrial mission and health care carried on by Friends in Kenya, East Africa. Friends do not ask about religious affiliations or political commitments when administering relief to victims of war, disease, and natural disaster, although they certainly hope their love and service will demonstrate an alternative way of life that will appeal to and finally prevail in the minds and hearts of the recipients.

This division between mission and service in the Society of Friends has been very unfortunate. Only in recent years have efforts been made to heal the differences by having workers in both enterprises meet and try to share and communicate. During the 1970s a series of Mission and Service Conferences (London in 1973; New Windsor, Maryland, in 1976; and Chiquimujla, Mexico, in 1979) brought together leading Quakers from both groups—for the first time in some cases. Although few concrete results came from those conferences, at least it was a start. Also, in recent years service-minded Friends have become acquainted with the Society's extensive mission work in Kenya, East Africa, and the result has been greater understanding and appreciation. In a number of instances Friends have begun to cross these barriers that have unhappily divided the Society of Friends.

Although important relief and service work continued throughout Friends' history, especially during wartime or natural catastrophes, it was toward the end of the nineteenth century that Friends in England began to develop a new concern for the social order and to address the social needs around them. At that time the whole climate of Quaker life and thought began to be influenced by a relatively young group of Friends who wanted to set a new agenda, highlighted by the Manchester Conference of Friends held in 1895. The aim was to be less bound by the evangelical theology of the past and more open to new attitudes toward science and religion, especially in the area of biblical interpretation. Persons such as Rendel Harris, Edward Grubb, John Wilhelm Rowntree, and William Charles Braithwaite on the British side, and Rufus Jones on the American side provided much of the impetus and leadership for this new mode of thought. Within ten years after the Manchester Conference, London Yearly Meeting turned a corner toward liberalism in faith and practice, rejecting much of the evangelical influence of the nineteenth century. In America similar movements were at work.

The impetus for Quaker service during the first half of the twentieth century derived largely from Friends' response to the problems of the First and Second World Wars and focused on two main concerns. The first stemmed from the Peace Testimony and concerned conscientious objectors to military service, many of whom sought alternative service under Friends auspices. The second concerned those people who had suffered the ravages of war. These were brought together through alternative service for conscientious objectors, so that they might undertake the war relief and service work that their consciences would allow them to do and still meet the requirements of the government during wartime.

In 1914 the Meeting for Sufferings of London Yearly Meeting established the War Victims Relief Committee, which began to organize relief work abroad. This was patterned after a similar committee by the same name that had been formed in 1871 to help rebuild villages and towns and provide relief following the Franco-Prussian War of 1870-71. They also had adopted the same red and black double star that Friends had used in 1871 as a symbol of their work. At the beginning of World War I the London Yearly Meeting for Sufferings also established an Emergency Committee to deal with "enemy aliens" living in England and caught in the war situation. Another Quaker-sponsored program was the Friends Ambulance Unit, also formed at the beginning of the war, which served in Flanders, France, and Italy. However, it was not officially under the auspices of Friends and included many non-Friends as workers.

In the United States, Friends organized the American Friends Service Committee shortly after the U.S. entered the war in 1917. A program was set up at Haverford College near Philadelphia where conscientious objectors were trained for relief and reconstruction work. Rufus M. Jones, then professor of philosophy at Haverford College, was the leader in these beginning years of the AFSC; Henry Cadbury and others were also involved. A. Ruth Fry, in her description of Quaker relief work during that period, reports that in 1918-19 more than five hundred English and American men and women were trained and sent into Quaker relief centers; and over twice that number served on relief and reconstruction projects in France during the 1914-1920 period.[15] Friends relief and reconstruction work continued in war-torn areas into the 1920s, long after the Armistice was signed, including many countries in Western Europe as well as Poland and Russia.

A long-term service project that Friends became involved in was the establishment of Friends International Centres in more than a dozen major cities around the world. This began as a vision of Carl Heath, who wanted to establish "Quaker embassies" in the major capitol cities of Europe. Through the influence of Heath and others a number of such centres came into being to serve as listening posts and outlets for Quaker service on a more permanent basis. In 1918 these centres came under the care of the Council for International Service at Friends House in London, which was the successor to the Friends War Victims Relief Committee; then in 1927 it merged with the Friends Foreign Missionary Association to form the Friends Service Council (later changed to Quaker Peace and Service) of London Yearly Meeting. The American Friends Service Committee also joined in the support of these Friends International Centres.

Canadian Friends formed the Canadian Friends Service Committee, which together with the American Friends Service Committee, headquartered in Philadelphia, worked jointly with Quaker Peace and Service in London to carry out Quaker service work in the world. The success of this joint effort was marked by the awarding of the 1947 Nobel

Peace Prize to Friends through their two largest service bodies, AFSC in Philadelphia and FSC in London

The American Friends Service Committee has become a very large operation expanding far beyond what Jones, Cadbury and other Philadelphia Friends imagined in their original vision. It has some forty offices in nine regions in the U.S., though its work is worldwide in scope, and the annual budget exceeds $35 million, more than two-thirds of which is used for domestic projects and programs. Through the years, the number of workers, including volunteers, has ranged from four hundred to one thousand, depending on program needs. The programs of the AFSC are organized and implemented through three units, Peace Building, Community Relations, and International. The Committee is under the oversight of a forty-member board of directors appointed by a corporation, which in turn is made up of Quaker members at large, and of Quakers appointed by twenty-four Friends yearly meetings.

In addition to relief, rehabilitation, and refugee work after World War I, the early AFSC became involved with impoverished coal miners, self-help housing, work camps, peace caravans, and the Mexican program. During World War II it helped to run the Civilian Public Service Camps for conscientious objectors. Today the work of AFSC covers a variety of issues and projects in peace and justice ranging from militarism and disarmament in Peace Building; race, economic justice, minority rights, sexism and criminal justice in Community Relations; to development, community building, and trans-national services in International. The longstanding Quaker International Affairs work, closely allied with the Quaker United Nations Program, continues to pursue quiet diplomacy, without portfolio, in significant trouble spots in the world. Areas of the world where AFSC has had special focus have included Southeast and Northeast Asia, Southern Africa, the Middle East and Latin America. In addition, there have been the Quaker

United Nations program in New York, the Washington Seminar Program, and the Diplomats Seminars abroad. This still does not tell the whole story of the AFSC, but it provides an overview and stresses the comprehensive nature of Quaker service.

An offshoot from the AFSC, although not a part of it, was the organization of the Friends Committee on National Legislation in Washington, D. C. in the midst of World War II (1943). This is the legislative and lobbying arm of Friends, which has worked for peace and justice in a wide range of issues involving government policy and legislation in the Congress. To this day it continues to offer a vigorous Quaker presence in the nation's capitol and has supplemented the tax-exempt work of AFSC on peace and justice concerns.

Quaker Education

The final form of Quaker outreach we shall look at is Friends significant involvement in education. It is sometimes assumed that because George Fox did not believe that persons could become ministers of Christ simply by being trained at Oxford or Cambridge, therefore he was opposed to education in general. This clearly was not the case. Those who have written on Quaker education in recent years have pointed out Fox's commitment to establishing schools for the youth.[17] It is also clear, however, that his concern for education had to do with "whatsoever things are civil and useful in creation."[18] This was basically a practical education in the skills of reading, writing, arithmetic, and geography. He also had a strong interest in instructing children so they would better understand and cope with the natural world. It is reported in the London Yearly Meeting Epistle of 1695 "that Schools and Schoolmasters who are faithful Friends and well-qualified, be placed and encouraged in all Counties, Cities, Great Towns or places where there may be need."[19]

Friends very early established what we would call elementary and secondary schools in both England and America. These were private schools under the care of particular monthly meetings in the case of elementary education, and under the care of yearly meetings in the case of secondary education. For the most part the latter became boarding schools where children lived as a family, usually with a superintendent and matron serving as surrogate parents for the children away from home. Thus family life was fostered as an important part of Quaker education.

Because early Friends were barred from the universities in England, as was true of Nonconformists in general, we might suppose they would have been keen to establish their own institutions of higher education. That this was not the case again indicates their emphasis on practical and functional education for children. It has been pointed out, however, that because some of the early Quaker leaders, such as Penington, Barclay, and Penn, had been well schooled themselves, they did not readily sense the needs of others who had been deprived of advanced education. It was not until the nineteenth century that Friends in the U.S. began experimenting with higher education.

In a chapter on Quaker education, Elbert Russell's *History of Quakerism* points out that Friends were not only denied a college or university education because of their nonconformist stance, but failed to provide adequate religious education for their children. This was primarily because Friends believed that religion had to be experienced and not taught. It was customary in Friends schools to have daily Bible reading and worship, but formal religious instruction as such was not undertaken because such instruction was regarded as "creaturely activity," especially during the Quietistic period of Quakerism in the eighteenth century. Friends were to turn to the Inward Teacher for guidance and instruction.

As Friends emerged from the Quietism of the eighteenth century they began to sense the need for more education, and after the British Reform Act of 1832 they were permitted to attend the universities. In America it was not long before Friends began to turn their boarding schools into colleges (such as Haverford in 1856, Earlham in 1859, and Guilford in 1888), while the addition of formal religious education in this century was a result of the influence of the Sunday school movement. In such ways were Friends in America indirectly influenced by outside forces in church and society.

Friends have always been experimental and innovative, and this has certainly been true in education. One such experiment (referred to early in this chapter) was begun by John Bellers in the suburbs of London in 1695. His aim was to form work colonies of poor people who were to be taught while engaged in industrial and agricultural pursuits. Although the experiment was not successful for efficiency reasons, some of the basic ideas were later used in the founding of Saffron Walden Friends School at Essex in 1702.

Another experiment was carried on by the innovative Joseph Lancaster (also referred to earlier) who used a teaching method called the monitorial system, where older and more mature students served as instructors for the younger ones. The aim was to provide an inexpensive education for the poorer classes. Lancaster was not a good manager, but his idea formed the basis for a popular education movement in Great Britain, where until the middle of the nineteenth century education was for the privileged aristocracy only.

A third experiment was the Adult School Movement in England, which began in 1845, though its antecedents dated back fifty years before that. It also was aimed at the less privileged classes before universal education was available to them. At the start the Adult Schools consisted largely of Sunday morning Bible study classes and discussion groups for working class people. Later they were broadened into a non-sectarian educational movement which taught simple skills of reading and writing. Joseph Sturge, William White, and George Cadbury of Birmingham all became promoters and benefactors of the movement, and White devoted most of his life to the work. Late in the nineteenth century the Adult Schools became the base for liberal religious teaching and concern for the social and industrial order. It was in part through the influence of this movement that membership in London Yearly Meeting grew significantly toward the end of century.

On the American side, schools were established wherever Friends settled. Many monthly meetings had their own elementary schools; in the East they established boarding schools on a secondary level; and in the Midwest and West they established Quaker academies which flourished in the nineteenth century. Later these were taken over by local communities and integrated with the public school system. During the nineteenth century Friends established a dozen colleges, sometimes evolving out of their boarding schools and Bible colleges (for example, Cleveland Bible College is now Malone College, and Friends Bible College in Kansas is now Barclay College). Quakers also had a strong influence on the development of both public and private universities.[20] All in all, Friends in North America have over eighty schools under their care, including all levels from elementary through college.[21]

The latest development in Quaker education has been primarily a twentieth century phenomenon—namely, the establishment of adult and graduate study centers. The first of these was Woodbrooke College in Birmingham, England, established in 1903. This resulted from a series of summer schools sparked by the Manchester Conference of 1895, the first of which was held at Scarborough in 1897. By 1900 a similar set of summer schools was started in the Philadelphia area, culminating in the Woolman School in 1915. This effort eventually led to the establishment of Pendle Hill at Wallingford, Pennsylvania, in 1930. Both Woodbrooke and Pendle Hill are religious and social study centers but do not ordinarily grant degrees. The first fully accredited degree-granting Friends graduate school was the Earlham School of Religion established at Richmond, Indiana, in 1960, affiliated with Earlham College. In subsequent years three other Friends graduate seminaries have been added by Western Friends: Houston Theological Seminary in Texas, Friends Center at Azusa Pacific University near Los Angeles, California, and George Fox Evangelical Seminary in Portland Oregon, affiliated with George Fox University at Newberg, Oregon.

Quaker education continues to be a growing phenomenon, although the number of Friends students is decreasing as compared with the non-Friends in most Quaker schools. A recent trend is for monthly meetings to establish elementary as well as pre-elementary schools to serve nursery and kindergarten children, while some Quaker families are preferring to home school their children. Another development is the formation of two national Quaker organizations that service Quaker schools: the Friends Council on Education, which oversees the interests of lower schools through senior high, and the Friends Association for Higher Education, which is a coordinating body for Friends colleges and for Quaker teachers in non-Quaker colleges and universities. Thus Quaker education continues to be a major form of outreach and service to society at large as well as to the Society of Friends.

Questions for Discussion

1. Have Friends a message to proclaim and share in word and deed? If so, how would you articulate it?
2. Is the Quaker message universal for all people, or is it intended to appeal to a limited few?
3. How do you account for the extraordinary zeal Friends have had for service to those in need all over the world?
4. How has Friends' missionary work of the nineteenth and twentieth centuries differed from that of the early missionary endeavors of the "valiant sixty"?
5. Why has there been such a division between mission and service-minded Friends?
6. How can one account for the heavy involvement and investment of Quakers in education?

Quaker Assessment and Future Prospects

Recently a valued and knowledgeable Friend said to me: "Quakerism is here to stay, but the Society of Friends may be expendable." What he meant was that the essential message of Quakerism is valid and continues to offer hope for people seeking spiritual direction and a faith to live by, but the particular institutional organization known as the Religious Society of Friends may not survive in its present form as a vehicle for proclaiming and living out that faith and message.

It is often said that institutions never die, or else they die hard. People cling to them for sentimental reasons or out of habit, both of which may run contrary to reason. When this happens stagnation occurs or rigor mortis sets in and the institution dies. I certainly hope that the Society of Friends has not reached either of these points, although sometimes its future seems uncertain and precarious.

Periodically Friends examine themselves and speculate about their future. Every few years some individual or organization comes out with a statement or pamphlet about "The Future of Quakerism," and the constant watchword is a call for "renewal." What this actually means is never clearly defined; but there is always an assumption that the Society of Friends has seen better days and the wish that we could somehow bring the present alive in the way it was at the beginning. Is this merely nostalgia for the past, or were there times when Friends truly lived in accordance with George Fox's vision?

Friends take an unusual interest in their own history. Upon becoming acquainted with Friends in his town, a Presbyterian minister was heard to ask: "Why are Quakers so interested in their history? Presbyterians have no such interest in their history." I think part of the explanation lies in the fact that Friends have no creeds to provide an anchor and guideline for their life together; therefore, they keep their traditions alive by telling their story over and over again, which provides a reference point that is equivalent to the creeds for many denominations. Unfortunately this preoccupation with their story also has a down side; by wallowing in their history Friends lose the ability to live into the future.

Quakerism: Sect, Movement or Denomination?

In 1945 Rufus M. Jones gave the Johnson Lecture at the Five Years Meeting of Friends (now Friends United Meeting) entitled "Original Quakerism, a Movement, Not a Sect." In explaining his premise, he said:

By *Sect* I mean, of course, as the word implies, a "branch" or "member" of the total Christian Body, a fragment separated and cut apart from the Great Church, which is rightly called the "Catholic," that is, Universal, Church. Sectarianism always spells failure in religion. A Sect is always a broken fragment, not a vital whole. By *Movement* I mean the growth and unfolding of a seed-principle, that has within it an inward power of expansion, a capacity of continually attracting adherents, a contagious tendency of enlarging its area and a tendency to resist rigid and static forms, which involve arrested development. [1]

Jones concluded that from the beginning Quakerism was intended to be a movement—a movement "of the one true Universal Church of the living God."

George Fox and his circle of Friends knew only too well that they were merely a remnant, a small fellowship in a great world, but he lived and died in the faith that the Quaker group was the *Seed* of an immense world-wide harvest that would, he believed, eventually become universal. [2]

Although Quakerism began as a movement, by the nineteenth century a majority of the Orthodox body of Friends had moved away from historic Quaker practices and closer to mainstream Protestant Christianity. In doing so, Friends in the Gurney pastoral tradition assumed many of the characteristics of denominationalism. Timothy Terrell maintains "that the Orthodox Quakers in America eventually conformed to the American religious mainstream and moved from a sectarian social orientation to a denominational orientation." [3] The outward expressions of Quakerism in worship, ministry, and mission took on many of the characteristics of the Protestant denominations, and Friends began to lose their distinctive marks as "a peculiar people" attempting to recover and live out first-century Christianity. Friends gave up some of the disciplinary standards of the past and gained tolerance and openness toward other Christian denominations, tending toward the American cultural pattern of individualism. [4]

In 1895 the Manchester Conference of Friends in England challenged the evangelicalism of the Gurney tradition in favor of a more liberal and open expression of Quakerism espoused by John Wilhelm Rowntree and, later, by Rufus M. Jones in America. Meanwhile, the Hicksite tradition of Friends began to emerge with an identity of its own at the turn of the century. These new patterns of Quakerism were eventually given organizational expression. In the twentieth century a strong denominational emphasis has taken form, while sectarianism has often characterized much of liberal Quakerism, as well as the small body of Conservative (Wilburite) Friends.

Some classify Quakers as mavericks when trying to decide where they fit in the history of the Christian tradition. Earlier we mentioned that some have held that Friends are neither Protestant nor Roman Catholic but represent a third form of Christianity in faith and practice. But the largest group of Friends, the Orthodox body, moved away from the sectarian tradition and increasingly conformed to American Protestant Christianity and denominationalism. And while the Hicksite and Wilburite Friends remained more sectarian, some liberal yearly meetings (such as Philadelphia) associated themselves with the ecumenical work of the National and World Councils of Churches. Eventually Friends General Conference and Friends United Meeting joined in these ecumenical relations, as did Canadian and London Yearly Meetings in observer status. So although Friends have always aspired to remain a religious movement, in Jones's definition of that term, the fact is that they have sometimes looked and acted more like a sect or a denomination than a movement.

It is instructive that two twentieth-century students of Quakerism as different in approach as Rufus Jones and Lewis Benson agreed that Fox and early Friends had a universal message. Benson's most important articulation of this is his book, *Catholic Quakerism*, where he spells out what he believes was Fox's vision. Concerning its universal message he writes:

The early Friends claimed that the truth that had been given them to proclaim was universal and that their faith was a catholic faith which was for all men to share. It is my aim to set forth the case for catholic Quakerism and to examine the foundations on which it was based.[5]

Jones expressed his understanding of the early Quaker universal view in this way:

I should like to see once more, as at the birth of our own Quaker movement, that faith and that hope spring up in our Society of Friends that we were the bearers of the seed of a Universal Church of the Spirit. I wish we might have in our lives the reality of experience, the measure of dedication, the depth of love, the Christlike spirit, the mark of the Galilean accent, that would make all Christians of all types feel that here, in this type of life, is a real model of a Christianity that could be universalized. Then whether we survived as a denomination or not would not too greatly matter, if only we could transmit a contagious spirit and way of life which had in it the length and breadth and depth and height of a Universal Church of Christ.[6]

Jones concludes his plea for Quakerism as a universal movement with these words:

All too long we as a people have been content to be a sect. The time has come to recover the vision of our forefathers and inaugurate once more a movement toward a type of Christianity, which might well become a universal faith.[7]

Appraisal of Friends Today

Whenever one tries to evaluate Friends in terms of numbers, the results are never very encouraging. According to the 1997 membership count there were 281,860 Friends in the world, 95,943 of whom live in North America (chiefly in the U.S.). The comparable count for thirty years ago was 193,800 in the world and 122,660 in North America.[8] So there has been a decline in North America while the primary growth areas have been Third World countries where Friends' missions have gone. The latter is especially true of Kenya, East Africa; among the Aymara Indians in Bolivia and Peru; and in Taiwan and India. The Kenya figure of 92,672 members, included in the above total, is probably understated; it is likely that more than 100,000 would be accurate if attenders are included. Bolivian and Peruvian Friends have doubled in the past few years, probably now approaching 25,000 or more. And in Taiwan membership grew from 30 to 3,000 in a ten-year period.[9]

England and America, the traditional home of Quakerism, clearly do not represent the growing edge. In the United States a substantial number of new meetings have been started around college and university campuses, most of which are small unprogrammed meetings. A few new and growing pastoral meetings have developed among evangelical Friends, and in those cases the membership is often in the hundreds, with two Sunday morning services. In spite of these signs of growth, the general picture of Friends in America is one of numerical decline. So if Friends have a future, we cannot rely on head count to determine what that future will be. There must be other things of significance to keep the Quaker witness alive.

A second way to appraise Friends is to look at their polarity of diversity and unity. There is no dispute about the great diversity of

Friends today, and in extreme cases this has taken the form of unchecked individualism with little sense of what our identity is as a community of faith and practice. Even in the beginning years of the Quaker movement Friends had to deal with diversity and division. In the eighteenth century the elders tried to quell diversity through disciplinary action. As a result Friends were disowned almost indiscriminately for a broad range of reasons, some of which would be questioned by Friends today.[10] In the nineteenth century attitudes toward diversity hardened into not only disownment of individuals, but major separations of Friends along yearly meeting lines.

The tolerance of Friends for diversity has greatly increased in this century. This is especially true of those of liberal persuasion, even to the point of welcoming, if not encouraging, tolerance and diversity. On the other hand, although evangelical Friends are now more willing to cooperate and communicate with Friends of other persuasions, the conservatives among them would like to unite Friends under one statement of faith, which would inevitably exclude many who could not subscribe to such a doctrinal position. Although there seems to be greater openness and communication among Friends of all persuasions, there are still deep divisions along doctrinal lines as well as in life-style and attitudes toward the world.

While there has been some movement toward greater unity in recent years, new issues have arisen to cause controversy and division. There is the Quaker Universalist movement, for example, which regards historic Christ-centered Quakerism as too narrow in a world where we need to join hands with persons of other religious faiths. They see Quakerism as a bridge to these people, as expressed in the commitment to "that of God in every one."

Two other areas of diversity and controversy are the feminist movement and the gay and lesbian movement. Although Friends have always espoused the equality of women and men, Quaker practice has not always kept up with this profession; coupled with this is the problem of sexist language which has seemed to regard women as second class to their male counterparts. The homosexual issue involves not whether we accept such persons in their own right but whether we expect of them a standard of behavior superior to that of heterosexuals. Even more divisive is the question of same-gender marriages under the care of the meeting, which suggests a pattern of sexual morality and family life unacceptable to the majority of Friends. So the issues dividing Friends today are not just the traditional ones of peace and justice and whether social change requires direct social action or whether the slower method of social change by education is the Quaker way. New problems and new challenges confront each new generation of Friends to further complicate the diversity/unity issue. As long as these matters persist there is little sign of Friends becoming united into a family governed by love, respect, and compassion for one another.

Efforts to Bring Friends Together

The Richmond Conference of Friends in 1887, which produced the controversial Richmond Declaration of Faith, was an attempt to unite all Orthodox Friends in England and America.[11] Then in 1895 the Manchester Conference of Friends was held in Manchester, England, to inaugurate a new and fresh approach to Quaker faith and life in the British Isles.[12] This movement was led by the youthful and vibrant John Wilhelm Rowntree, and the intention was to set in motion an alternative to the century-old evangelical orientation of British Quakerism. On the American side this new approach to Quakerism was picked up by Rufus Jones who subsequently articulated liberal Quakerism on both sides of the Atlantic.

With the coming of World War I and the concern of Friends to provide alternative service for conscientious objectors, far-reaching peace and service work became institutionalized in the American Friends Service Committee and its British counterpart, the Friends Service Council. The service work of Friends spearheaded an effort to unite Friends in service and action rather than focus on doctrinal unity. In the aftermath of the war the first All-Friends Conference was held in London in 1920. Thus Friends working and consulting together led to the first World Conference of Friends at Haverford and Swarthmore Colleges in Pennsylvania in 1937, where the Friends World Committee for Consultation was launched. The Friends World Committee has been instrumental in sponsoring subsequent world conferences (1952 Oxford, England and 1967 Guilford College, NC) and triennial gatherings in many countries of the world. FWCC has also supported inter-visitation among Friends and sponsored of Quaker Youth Pilgrimages in Europe and America.

Other developments in this century have brought better understanding and unity among Friends, such as the experiences of conscientious objectors during World War II, particularly the Civilian Public Service alternative service camps and projects sponsored by the Historic Peace Churches in the U.S., including the AFSC-CPS camps for the Friends. Many young men from the various branches of Friends met and learned to respect and accept each other despite their Quaker differences and organizational divisions.

Despite intermittent periods of weakness or low activity, the Young Friends Movement has strengthened the ties among various kinds of Friends through the years. In the post–World War II period the Young Friends of North America inherited these cross-cultural inter-yearly meeting gatherings of Friends, although its activities have appealed mostly to liberal Friends rather than evangelicals. The latter have sponsored alternative gatherings called "Youth Quake," which have met periodically at various locations. The most notable recent activity of young Friends was the World Conference of Young Friends held at Guilford College in 1985. This was well attended by many kinds of Friends from around the world and resulted in a sobering but searching experience for those who may become future leaders of the Society. Many were surprised by their first encounter with the wide diversity of Friends both in faith and practice.

Another significant gathering of Friends was the First International Theological Conference of Quaker Women held at Woodbrooke College, Birmingham, England in 1990. Seventy-four women from twenty-one countries representing many races, languages, faith orientations and practices came together to share their stories. Their epistle at the end says they felt "called into wholeness and into community" where they are in their homes, meetings/churches, and work places.

Also important in the life of Friends has been the chance to meet others of like mind or of differing views at conferences and retreat centers. Among the most successful of these have been Powell House at Old Chatham, New York, under the care of New York Yearly Meeting, and Quaker Hill Conference Center at Richmond, Indiana. The latter for ten years co-sponsored with the Earlham School of Religion an annual Friends Consultation of Fifty Friends from twenty or more states and from twenty or more yearly meetings, including Canadian and London Yearly Meetings. These consultations have covered a wide range of issues of importance to the local meeting, providing occasions for Friends of differing persuasions to discover each other at a deep spiritual level.

During the 1970s a series of Faith and Life Conferences took place among all branches of Friends in the United States. Initially two national conferences were held at St. Louis (1970) and Indianapolis

(1974), which led to a series of smaller regional conferences. At the Indianapolis Conference all yearly meetings in the U.S. were represented for the first time, except for Central Yearly Meeting, which sent observers. Again, Friends were able to communicate across divisions of the past, something that would hardly have seemed possible a few years earlier.

Among pastoral Friends there has been a series of important pastors conferences over the past quarter of a century. Begun in Dallas, Texas, in 1976 (followed by St. Louis in 1980, Chicago in 1985, Denver in 1989, Orlando, Florida in 1999 and Atlanta, GA in 2000), these conferences have brought together Quaker leadership across yearly meeting lines, including persons from Friends United Meeting and Evangelical Friends International.

Also of significance have been spinoffs from the educational work of Friends to help Quakers dialogue together and confront their differences. Most important have been the contributions of three Quaker post-graduate centers referred to earlier (page 180): Woodbrooke College in Birmingham, England (founded in 1903), Pendle Hill near Philadelphia, Pennsylvania (1930), and the Earlham School of Religion, Richmond, Indiana (1960). All of these schools have emphasized the Quaker dimension of their educational programs, and all have attempted to draw students from an ecumenical Quaker mix. Some of the Friends colleges have also facilitated such inter-Quaker and inter-yearly meeting dialogues, the most notable currently being the Friends Center at Guilford College, North Carolina, and The Thomas Kelly Center at Wilmington College, Wilmington, Ohio. George Fox University, Friends University, and William Penn University have also interacted in positive ways with Friends in their yearly meetings and regions. On a national level in the U.S. two Friends organizations have held significant educational conferences—Friends Council on Education for Quaker Secondary Schools, and Friends Association for Higher Education.

Growing out of his experience at Earlham School of Religion, Samuel Caldwell, General Secretary of Philadelphia Yearly Meeting, launched in the 1980s a Quaker Studies Program in his yearly meeting. The core curriculum included Bible Study, History of Christian Thought, and Quakerism, and the program met with good response and has since spread to other yearly meetings. It is significant that all of these Quaker study efforts are reinstituting Bible study with a significant and positive response from Friends. Although conservative and evangelical Friends have always had a strong biblical orientation, liberal Friends have often lost touch with the biblical sources of Quakerism so that there is a need to recover those particular roots.

In summation, all of these activities have helped Quakers bridge their differences and begin to communicate across the barriers of past separations.

Quaker Vision and Purpose

In light of all this, we need to look seriously at whether the Society of Friends has an identifiable purpose and message that will unite Friends in the future. Do Friends have a vision of their place in the world that brings them together at a deeper level than the organizational and institutional ties just mentioned? The answer to this question is of paramount importance if we take seriously the biblical claim that "where there is no vision, the people perish" (Prov. 29:18 KJV). If the Society of Friends suffers from a lack of such vision and sense of direction, then its future is problematic indeed.

It is my belief that Friends do have a unique witness to make in the world and that they have been called from the beginning to proclaim it.

And if Friends do have a distinctive understanding of the Gospel and its claims upon humankind, then we need to rediscover and re-articulate the content of that message. Let me quote from my pamphlet entitled *The Gospel According to Friends*:

> It would, of course, be unrealistic to suggest that Friends are yet ready to develop a common faith and practice in the light of our century and a half of separations and estrangements from one another. Moreover, Friends cherish their individual and corporate freedom too much to suggest or desire that degree of unity. But is it too much to hope that we can rediscover a common identity as a worldwide family of Friends with some common distinguishing features? And, in rediscovering this, cannot we hope to experience a new spiritual birth and effectiveness for our time? Is not the world eagerly awaiting this kind of spiritual renewal and leadership to come from Friends?[13]

If we are not able to agree on a common statement of our Quaker faith and practice, could we not address the question of a common Quaker purpose and message in another way? Certainly there are some religious and social testimonies in our history that have been normative in Friends faith and practice. By "normative" I mean that these testimonies can be objectively discerned and articulated because they have been so widely held and practiced for three hundred and fifty years that they have become a way of life for Friends and are often spoken of as "Friends principles." Of course the concept of normative Quakerism suggests an ethical note—namely, the sense of "ought" about believing and practicing these Quaker testimonies. But "normative" also suggests some latitude for those whose inward leadings of the Spirit do not bring them to the same place at the same time. While "normative" expresses a sense of "oughtness," it is also open to God's continuing revelation through new and fresh leadings of the Holy Spirit.

The Normative Testimonies of Friends

As has been pointed out before, the very concept of "testimony" is congenial to Friends, conveying a sacramental quality of an outward sign and witness to an inward spiritual leading and commitment. It is a testimony of the mind as well as the heart, and it is always open to new leadings and insights. For Friends it is walking in the Light with the expectation that new insights and understandings will be illuminated by that Light. Friends have always been careful to emphasize that revelation of God's will and truth to us humans is a continuing process, so that spiritual leadings and understandings are dynamic and changing rather than static and immutable.

Although we have heretofore devoted Chapter 8 to the Friends testimonies, we need to briefly summarize them again as the norms by which we as Quakers try to live our lives. These and perhaps others not yet named or discerned constitute the norms by which we test the level of our faithfulness to the Light of Christ manifested in our spiritual walk with God.

The Religious Testimonies

First among the *religious* testimonies is the belief that we can have direct and immediate access to the living God. In early Quakerism this was referred to as the "Light of Christ within" and was identified with the so-called "Quaker Text" in John 1:9 and the eternal *Logos* referred to in the Prologue to the Gospel of John. By this Light, it is believed, we can *know* the Truth and discern the will of God, and it is this Light that can show us evil and can turn us to the good.

If the Light is the first religious testimony of Friends, the second is that we can not only *know* the will of God but can, by God's grace, be enabled to *do* the will of God. This led to the early Quaker doctrine of Christian perfection, or what some twentieth–century Friends have called "holy obedience." Although Friends recognize the serious pull of sin and evil in our lives, there is the belief that we can, in the language of George Fox, "live in the power of the Lord" to overcome sin and evil and live up to the measure of the Light God has given us.

A third religious testimony is the Quaker experience of community as expressed in the "gathered meeting." This is the concept of the church as the gathered fellowship of worshipers wherein we are members one of another and our individualism is disciplined and tested by the community of faith. Living in community also calls us to exercise responsibility and accountability in our relationships with one another.

A fourth Quaker religious testimony is the sacramental view of life. Friends believe that all of life is potentially holy and can serve as a means of God's grace. Every meal—not just the Lord's Supper—can be a sacramental meal. Friends also believe that our visible lives must become outward expressions and reflections of the inward life of the Spirit. Thus the admonition attributed to George Fox applies here: "Let your lives speak."

The Social Testimonies

In turning to the Quaker *social* testimonies, we are not saying that there are not other Quaker religious testimonies, or that they might not be expressed in ways other than those stated here. Also, in reality Friends would not want to separate the religious from the social; the two are organically related and dependent upon each other. The social is rooted in the religious while the social gives expression to the religious.

The best known social testimony is the Peace Testimony. For

Friends this is not just the absence of war and violence; it is a way of life that tries to embody the way of peace and justice in personal relationships and in the structures of society. Thus, the Peace Testimony is not just inward peace of mind and spirit, but must find expression in dealing with conflict in the outward affairs of the family, community, nation, and world.

Simplicity is a second social testimony—namely, that one's style and manner of living should be based on need, with a concern for the lives of others as reflected in the preservation and sharing of natural and human resources. Concern for simplicity may also require us to uncomplicate our lives by prioritizing what we do in terms of the values and testimonies we hold to be most important.

A third social testimony is equality—namely, that we hold all persons to be potentially of equal worth before God and therefore all should be treated with love and concern regardless of race, gender, creed, or social standing.

A fourth social testimony is integrity, which calls for truth-telling in all our relationships. It also calls for us to be persons of honesty and authenticity in our own personhood and for a consistency between our religious faith and the way we live.

Again, this is not an exhaustive list of testimonies, and Friends from various Quaker backgrounds and traditions might express them differently; but it is hoped that no Friend would disavow any of these basic principles of faith and practice. In this sense they might well serve as normative tests for living out our faith. They provide a functional anchor or an objective referent point. Like all human beings, Friends do not always live up to the measure of the Light that is given them, but these norms provide some spiritual and practical guidelines. Friends believe deeply that if they submit themselves to God and live by the Light of Christ they will be enabled to live by the truth of the Gospel.

Where Do We Go from Here?

Although the Quaker vision, as expressed in its purpose and message, may not always be as clear as it should be, it still has relevance and power to speak a prophetic word to the needs of our time. At the 1967 Friends World Conference at Guilford College, Hugh Doncaster declared that he believed the world was dying for lack of Quakerism in action.[14] Clearly our world is greatly in need of a Gospel of hope to be proclaimed, and I believe that Friends could be the bearers of such a message. But how can we get our act together to proclaim this message while the Society of Friends is plagued with so much diversity that we seem unable to act and speak with a common voice?

So the immediate question for us is whether there is any way forward that can accommodate and utilize the diversity, commitment, loyalty, and enthusiasm of all Friends? What follows is not a clear answer to this question, but perhaps this partial response will indicate some of the possibilities, as well as the hazards, of our moving ahead in unison as a Society of Friends.

Thirty years ago one of our elder statesmen, the late Everett Cattell, made some bold proposals for ways in which disunited Friends might find each other and work together. He set this forth in an article in a 1966 issue of *Quaker Religious Thought*, and he spelled it out more fully in an address to the 1970 Faith and Life Conference.[15] He called most attempts to bring Friends together "synthetic" and "artificial." This approach, he thought, inevitably forces Friends to unite unnaturally on a "least-common-denominator synthesis."[16] He then expressed his alternative proposal—a "symbiotic" approach based on a biological model:

In symbiosis the two organisms which live in proximity to each other still maintain their identity and biological integrity. The relationship between the two may vary in three ways. It may be *commensal* in that both feed from the same source but neither help nor disturb the other. It may be *mutual* in that each helps the other as for instance do ants and aphids. Or it may be *parasitical* where one benefits from the other and usually at its expense.[17]

Cattell proposed the possibility of the realignment of Friends in America on the symbiotic model of mutuality. He said this was not ideal and might in the end produce a schism, but he considered it a "live option," and "one hopes it can come with love and agreement." [18]

I believe Cattell's proposal for bringing Friends together into a working relationship deserves careful study and thought. Obviously if it were to happen it would mean a realignment of Friends into two main bodies, one evangelical and the other liberal. It would probably mean a revamping of Friends United Meeting and Evangelical Friends International into one organization to accommodate the evangelically oriented body of Friends, leaving Friends General Conference to be broadened into an organization to accommodate Friends of liberal persuasion. Among Conservative Friends, who are declining in number, some would probably be drawn to the evangelical side and some to the liberal side of realignment. Most independent yearly meetings would be drawn to the liberal orientation of Friends General Conference.

Granted that any further division of Friends is not desirable, I would like to suggest the following example as a model that might be workable and mutually beneficial on the way to greater unity. The two main bodies of Old Order Mennonites and General Conference Mennonites joined in the establishment of the Associated Mennonite Biblical Seminaries at Elkhart, Indiana, in 1969. The two bodies of Mennonites had already worked together in mission and service projects. The joint seminaries have had *two* presidents, one each for the two Mennonite constituencies for fund-raising and public relations purposes, but educationally they have had one dean, who serves the internal administrative needs of both schools. Now a further step has been taken in the appointment of one president for the two seminaries; thus, they operate as one seminary with two identifiable constituencies. On my sabbatical leave in 1979 I spent an entire semester at AMBS and continue to marvel at the way in which these two Mennonite bodies run one seminary with a united faculty and administration for the purpose of preparing pastoral leadership for their respective congregations. The success of this experiment with the seminaries has led to some long-term hopes and plans for the integration of these two Mennonite denominations, a proposal which is now in process.

Why could this organizational model not be applied to a realignment of Friends as suggested by Everett Cattell? There could be a united headquarters sharing many services of importance to both groups of Friends, perhaps with one or two satellite offices to serve the country geographically. This is not the place to spell out the details of such a symbiotic reorganization, but it has possibilities that could be explored to the benefit of all Friends in America. There is much that we can and could learn from each other. Neither the evangelical nor the liberal wing of Quakerdom represents the "pure stream" of the Religious Society of Friends; each represents a piece of the Quaker whole.

Let me add to this a relevant word about our experience at the development of the Earlham School of Religion, beginning in 1960. There is no other place in American Quakerdom where Friends of all persuasions have worked together over sustained periods of time as they have at ESR. It is true that the school has drawn few students from the extreme ends of the spectrum of evangelical/liberal Friends, but substantial numbers of moderate evangelicals and moderate liberals have lived, studied, and worked together in harmony and mutual respect; they have been able to rise to a new level of understanding and sharing of a common purpose and vision for the Society of Friends. Out of my own experience at ESR, I am convinced that Friends of differing persuasions can work together and learn from each other.

The main stumbling block to such progress is the increasing tension between Universalist Friends and those who are committed to a Christ-centered Quakerism. This is much more the case now than thirty years ago when Cattell ventured his proposal, saying in the same address: "No one has a right to use the word Quaker to describe a system which is not Christocentric." [19] Maurice Creasey defines the Universalist position as just the opposite: "Quakerism, according to this view, is accidentally rather than essentially Christian, or is only Christian in the sense that it seeks to base itself upon the 'simple teachings of Jesus'. . . ." [20]

At the turn of the twentieth century that remarkable young British Friend, John Wilhelm Rowntree, warned that "wild fantastic forms of thought from time to time run riot here and there [in the Society of Friends], for lack of a steadying central conception [of Quakerism]." [21] In reporting this, Creasey makes clear what John Wilhelm Rowntree meant by this "steadying central conception."

> The very heart and centre of the Quaker message was a rediscovery and a reaffirmation of the reality and sufficiency of the presence and power of Christ. And this presence and power were to be known in and expressed through a living, worshipping, gathered community, acknowledging Christ as Lord and Leader. A distinctive witness concerning the meaning of Christ and his Church—this, in a phrase, was where John Wilhelm Rowntree found the "steadying central conception" of Quakerism. [22]

As long as there is no resolution of this debate between Universalist Friends and Christocentric Friends, any revamping of Quakerism for the purpose of working toward greater unity seems fraught with difficulties.[23] But in spite of what might seem like a roadblock in our way, I would continue to assert the importance of proclaiming the historic Christian Quaker message set forth in this volume. Was not Hugh Doncaster right when he said that the world is dying for want of Quakerism in action? And I continue to be moved by the statement of Seth Hinshaw regarding the need to share the message: "Early Friends were people whose lives had been electrified by the power of the Living Christ, and who felt called and commissioned to go forth and change the world."[24] Whether we have this kind of zeal and whether we are up to the task before us is unclear. Perhaps in the service of such a cause we need to make ourselves expendable. For as Everett Cattell said: "The future of Friends may be like the grain of wheat which must fall into the ground and die. Perhaps this would be the way to a new harvest."[25]

Perhaps we need to experience a new sense of humility, vulnerability, and openness to what God needs to be doing through us. And if it is the Quaker vision and message that has validity, rather than the institutional structures of the Society of Friends, perhaps this essential and normative Quakerism that we have been talking about needs to be repackaged in new wineskins, recalling the parable of Jesus: "Neither is new wine put into old wineskins; if it is, the skins burst, and the wine is spilled, and the skins are destroyed; but new wine is put into fresh wineskins, and so both are preserved" (Matt. 9:17). I do believe we are heirs of a religious tradition as new and fresh as the day it was envisioned by George Fox. It is a Gospel of truth and love and hope, which also formed the essence of the message of Jesus. We need to find new ways of expressing it personally and corporately in today's world.

Leonard Kenworthy, in a 1984 lecture to Friends General Conference, said that "the Religious Society of Friends today is a little like a banked fire, with warm ashes, but in need of fresh kindling and some vigorous stirring. Perhaps God, The Great Blacksmith, needs to use His bellows on us."[26] Whatever figure of speech we use to express our desires and hopes for Friends, let us become expendable in the hands of God for the purpose of fulfilling God's purposes through us. In the light of this sense of calling and mission let us continue to ask these two questions:

—How can we express together the faith that has been entrusted to us as Friends?

—How can we give an account of the hope that is in us as Friends?[27]

An Emerging Quaker Spirituality

Some time ago I was talking with a thoughtful and perceptive young Friend who believes that there is "an emerging Quaker spirituality," which he has experienced among some Friends. If that is so, then perhaps that is the most promising sign of the future. No amount of "fixing" the Society will come to much unless there is an underlying spirituality that is alive and well, as we claim it was in the early days of the Quaker movement.

As one moves around among Friends there are signs of this spirituality, and where it appears it is indeed refreshing. But how widespread is this, and is it sufficient to make any claim for the future? Doubtless there have always been "alive" Friends and "alive" meetings. So is what we see today any different? Indeed the non-aliveness of so many Friends and their meetings causes one to be very cautious about forecasting the future. We may pray and we may hope, however, that this young Friend is right and that God may be ready to gather "a new people" in our day as "a great people" was gathered in George Fox's day. With this vision of hope let us dedicate ourselves to the vision of "an emerging spirituality" that has both temporal and eternal meaning, significance, and durability.

Questions for Discussion

1. Is Quakerism essentially a set of beliefs, a way of life, a method of discerning religious truth, or simply a personal religious experience?
2. Is the Society of Friends a sect, a movement, a church, or a denomination?
3. Is diversity an asset or a liability for Friends? And how can it be integrated into community?
4. Are there elements of faith and practice that all Friends share so that they might be able to speak with one voice? If so, what are they?
5. What new forms and structures are needed among Friends to give expression and meaning to our Quakerism?
6. In what sense have Friends been "a peculiar people" throughout their history? Should this image be preserved or abandoned?

Postscript

The purpose of this Postscript is to provide further commentary and background information on my book and how it came about. It has been in circulation now for ten years and significant feedback has been received along with helpful book reviews. I will give some new input as well as respond to some of the questions and criticisms.

When I was in seminary at Yale Divinity School in the late 1940s I enrolled in more than one Systematic Theology course with Professor Albert Outler. This was very helpful to me in trying to understand and make sense of my Christian faith. As a result I felt somebody needed to write a systematic theology of Quaker faith and religious beliefs. After teaching theology and Christian ethics, as well as Quakerism courses, at Earlham School of Religion for twenty-five years, I decided that perhaps I was the one to write such a book. So while I continued teaching another five years I drew heavily from my classroom experience with students as I began writing *A Living Faith: An Historical Study of Quaker Beliefs.*

But let me go farther back than that to the 1950s. After seminary I was further convinced that Friends needed to overcome their pejorative view of theology and theologizing. From their beginning Friends have been opposed to *creeds* about religious faith in place of direct *religious experience* of that faith. So sometimes they have condemned theological discourse as a denial of authentic religious faith and experience.

In 1957 I took the lead in helping form the Quaker Theological Discussion Group (QTDG), which had its beginnings at the Conference of Friends in the Americas at Wilmington College in Ohio. This group started meeting regularly every year and began publishing a theological journal, *Quaker Religious Thought* (QRT). It brought together Friends from diverse Quaker backgrounds for serious dialogue about Quaker theological issues. In recent years QTDG has met intermittently, but its publication *Quaker Religious Thought* has been consistently published three or four times a year since 1957. The editorship has been shared among the different branches of Friends geographically and with differing theological perspectives. There has been some criticism from the polar ends of the Quaker theological spectrum (fundamentalism to universalism) that their theological views have not been properly represented in the dialogue. Also in the beginning, some Friends who were not a part of QTDG looked askance at the entire enterprise as un-Quakerly, but gradually it became accepted, although not widely known among Friends. Through this Quaker theological fellowship we have gained respect for one another in spite of our Quaker differences. We have been able to agree and disagree in a good spirit — something which many believed could never happen. How much this effort has helped change the face of Quakerism in America is unknown, but indirectly it has had a positive influence toward helping to bridge Quaker theological differences. Thus "theology" is no longer censured and excised from the Quaker vocabulary.

Quaker Spirituality and Theological Language

At the very end of *A Living Faith* I very briefly spell out what I call "An Emerging Quaker Spirituality." What I was sensing then, ten years ago, continues to impress me today. Therefore, the possibility of a new spiritual formation among Friends is much in my thoughts as I write this Postscript.

Soon after the first edition of the book was published some friends obtained a copy and were trying to read it for their morning devotions. The impression I received was disappointment that the book did not seem to answer their need for spiritual devotion and prayer. My response of course was that it was not intended to be a devotional book. What I was trying to encourage was serious and thoughtful reflection on what Quakers believe and the faith basis for their belief. Therefore, I make no apologies for encouraging Friends to engage one another in theological reflection and discourse with the hope that it will be helpful in our spiritual journey together.

However, we should never overlook the constant need for a disciplined life of devotion to God in prayer, contemplation and quietly "waiting upon the Lord." Growth in the spiritual life cannot help but benefit from such a discipline on a daily basis, and prior to attending meeting for worship. There is no theological substitute for such a practice. Not only will one's personal life be enriched but the life of our meetings will benefit as well. What I mean by an "emerging Quaker spirituality" not only calls us to deepen the life of the Spirit, but we need to consider how our minds perceive and our speech imparts the spiritual meaning of our faith. Thus, the words we use to confess our faith and share with others is critically important.

Some Friends feel very uncomfortable with retaining the traditional Quaker and Christian words and phrases to describe their faith. These terms are usually understood and taken for granted by conservative and evangelical Friends but no longer seem relevant to many liberal Friends. Let me give a couple of examples. The word "prayer" is seldom heard or voiced in some Friends meetings. But at some point in the meeting for worship one or more persons will voice a concern to hold a certain person or situation in the Light. One cannot be quite sure whether it is "Light" with a capital "L", indicating that it comes from a Divine source, or merely a reflection of the natural sunlight coming through the meeting-house window? Apparently for some Friends "holding someone in the Light" seems more spiritual and acceptable than holding up that person in prayer to God. So is the problem the source of the Light, or is it our embarrassment about addressing God in prayer?

Another example is the meaning, and/or use, of the word "salvation" as a meaningful religious term. Again, persons in the conservative and more evangelical tradition know what this terms means whether or not it is frequently used. Among most liberal Friends one not only does not hear the word used, but apparently it has become meaningless unless one assumes there is such a thing as "sin" in our personal and corporate lives that needs to be addressed. Years ago I learned in my theological studies that the root meaning of salvation comes from the Latin "salvus," which means health and wholeness in contrast to a guilty conscience and fragmented life. Who among us does not want to be spiritually whole and healthy? Thus the need for theological definition and reflection on a whole series of words and phrases which are misunderstood or rejected in the language we use.

If indeed there is a spiritual stirring among us as Friends, can we dig a little deeper to better understand what we mean by "spiritual?" Even the words "spirit" and "spiritual" need to be carefully defined, because most of us would agree there are good spirits and evil spirits at play in us and in our world. I do not want to say our problem is simply semantics, namely, trying to discern the meaning of words. Rather, there are significant substantive questions at work, such as whether to capitalize a word to determine whether its source does or does not transcend our human and natural state of being. In other words, is there a spiritual reality beyond words but nevertheless meaningful to us?

Another spiritual concern we need to reflect on as Friends is a the distinction between "being" and "doing" in our lives. Most of our lives have been engaged in "doing," leaving very little time to nurture our "being," namely, who we are. It is important to remember that being and doing cannot and should not be kept in separate compartments. A well balanced life takes both seriously, but the truth that emerges is that we tend to be busy bodies "doing" without allowing enough time to nurture the spiritual "being" from which our "doing" should arise.

Response to Questions About A Living Faith, *1990 Edition*

The most formidable review of *A Living Faith: An Historical Study of What Quakers Believe* was by Arthur O. Roberts in *Quaker Religious Thought* #74, December, 1990, pp. 49-53. At that time he was Editor of *QRT* following a long career on the Religion and Philosophy faculty of George Fox College (now University) at Newberg, Oregon. The review, four-and-a-half pages long, prompted my response in *QRT* #78, July 1992, pp. 42-45. Although we came from quite different Quaker backgrounds and experiences, we have come to know each other through the Quaker Theological Discussion Group and other Quaker enterprises. We have often taken issue with each other but have maintained a relationship of respect and friendship. It is fitting, therefore, that this Postscript include references to his review of my book, and my corresponding responses.

Arthur Roberts gave a positive, thoughtful and affirmative review of the book, especially Chapters 3 through 8, but also raised some important questions. He spoke of the brevity of the book, which did not in some cases allow for a full treatment of certain Quaker theological issues. He questioned my use of the terms "evangelical" and "liberal" describing contemporary Friends in America without carefully defining the terms and indicating the metamorphosis through which they went. My response: "These terms ... lend themselves to a latitude of interpretation which call for greater precision. But any writer on theological topics is caught in a similar dilemma and finally has to apply labels whether or not they always fit.... Thus I contend that the evangelical/liberal labels are in a broad sense clear enough to convey significant meaning in theological discourse."

Arthur says "Cooper seems to imply that evangelicalism ... is a wild graft onto the Quaker tree whereas liberalism is a root stock growth, however much in need of pruning." He asks whether this was intended as a descriptive theological reference, or if it refers to the diverse forms of Quaker worship. Probably both meanings are intended, but my response is that contemporary Quaker liberalism is also theologically "a wild graft onto the Quaker tree" just as much as Quaker evangelicalism is in its departure from early forms of ministry, worship and church organization. In very different ways both types of Friends have departed from the vision of George Fox and early Friends.

Pointing out other deficiencies Arthur noted inadequate treatment of eschatology, millenarianism, authority of Spirit vs. Scripture, salvation and holiness, and the absolutist/relativist stand on the peace testimony. Admittedly these do call for fuller treatment, but I did not try to cover all the issues which might have appeared in a longer and more detailed volume. But where there is uneven or inadequate treatment I accept responsibility. In the case of Chapter 9, "Last Things and Eternal

Hope," for example, he notes a lack of historical development of the topic similar to what was given in other chapters.

Turning to Chapter 10 "Quaker Mission, Service and Outreach," this is the longest chapter in the book even though Arthur would like to have seen greater coverage. My response: Granted that there is much more to be said about these outward expressions of Quakerism, I would contend that my summary in the allotted space demonstrates very well the resiliency of Quaker outreach. Friends track record is remarkable, and what other religious body of comparable size can match it? It was not my purpose to write a definitive history of Quaker mission and service, but to show how the corporate Quaker message and witness work themselves out in the world. (See *QRT* #78 p. 44)

One surprise in Arthur Roberts' review was his reference to my Conservative Friends background and its influence on my interpretation of Quaker faith and practice. I willingly acknowledge that it influenced my life, but my Conservative Friends family and friends think I short circuited them in *A Living Faith.* My most recent book, *Growing Up Plain: The Journey of a Public Friend (1999)* is an attempt to give a balanced view of how much I have been influenced by that tradition. H. Larry Ingle probably had it right in *QRT* #75, *1991, pp, 45-46* when he suggested that the writings of both Arthur Roberts and Wilmer Cooper reflect the influence of their respective Quaker heritage.

There is an area where Arthur and I give a slightly different reading to late nineteenth-century Quaker history. He has a faith-based positive reading of the 1887 Richmond (Indiana) Declaration of Faith. My experience is that in some quarters at least it has been controversial and divisive as compared with the unifying affects it was intended to have. Paradoxically he chides me for my essentially positive reaction to the noted Manchester Conference of 1895, attended by mostly British

Friends. Reflecting now on this, my observation is that both Arthur and I have over the years moved to a more centrist position theologically. But we view these two pacesetting Quaker conferences through different lenses.

The most controversial chapter of my book was Chapter 11 on "Quaker Assessment and Future Prospects," especially pp. 159-162. This deals with our Quaker diversity and how we might reorganize ourselves to work more amicably together on those things we can agree on, but continue along separate tracks where we do not agree. I had taken advantage of an earlier proposal by the respected evangelical Friends, Everett Cattell, which suggested a "symbiotic biological model" for organization as a way forward for Friends. This seemed important enough to Arthur Roberts that in his review of my book, and as Editor of *QTR* , he invited correspondence about the realignment proposal. But just as my book came out there was unbeknown to me another realignment proposal floating around which latched onto my reference to Everett Cattell's "symbiotic model" as a way for Friends to accommodate their differences. The trouble was that our two proposals, in terms of implementation, were quite different. At the time I predicted that the other approach to implementing realignment was doomed to failure, which is what happened.

Because of the importance of this realignment subject I had a hard time disassociating myself from the other realignment proposal. My response: "When I wrote *A Living Faith I* had no idea that the realignment of Friends would be a burning issue by the time the book came out. Had I foreseen this I would have written more fully about the proposal than pp. 159-161. When the storm of discussion was gathering ... I felt constrained to explain my views, which appeared in *Quaker Life*, July-August, 1991, pp. 44-45." My main point there was that for meaningful and peaceful realignment (though not without pain), there needed to be across-the-board consultations among all branches of Friends before a plan was devised and launched. The objective should be to determine what things we can do together as Friends as compared to those we are not yet ready to join together. I provided a couple of models for this and offered the belief that we could discover a new "symbiotic" working relationship similar to that suggested by Everett Cattell (see *QRT* #78, July 1992, pp. 44-45). In this new edition of *A Living Faith* which you are reading I have not changed the original text and believe the Everett Cattell proposal (as I interpreted it) still has validity, though it would not be an altogether happy solution to our Quaker struggles to reconcile each other's differences.

APPENDIX A

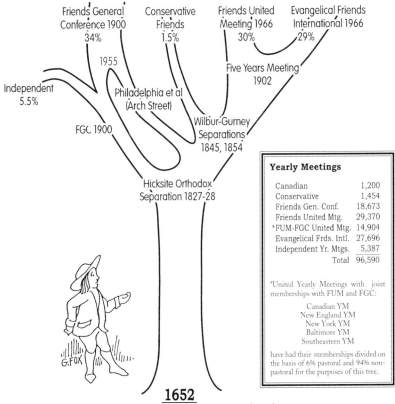

NORTH AMERICAN QUAKER TREE

NON-PASTORAL 39.5%   PASTORAL MEETINGS 60.5%

Friends General Conference 1900 34%

Conservative Friends 1.5%

Friends United Meeting 1966 30%

Evangelical Friends International 1966 29%

1955

Independent 5.5%

Philadelphia et al (Arch Street)

Five Years Meeting 1902

FGC 1900

Wilbur-Gurney Separations 1845, 1854

Hicksite Orthodox Separation 1827-28

G.FOX

Yearly Meetings

Canadian	1,200
Conservative	1,454
Friends Gen. Conf.	18,673
Friends United Mtg.	29,370
*FUM-FGC United Mtg.	14,904
Evangelical Frds. Intl.	27,696
Independent Yr. Mtgs.	5,387
Total	96,590

*United Yearly Meetings with joint memberships with FUM and FGC:

Canadian YM
New England YM
New York YM
Baltimore YM
Southeastern YM

have had their memberships divided on the basis of 6% pastoral and 94% non-pastoral for the purposes of this tree.

1652
Roots In 17th Century England

By Ed Nicholson - using October 2000 statistics provided by
Friends World Committee for Consultation

APPENDIX B

World Membership of Friends

According to statistics gathered by the Friends World Committee for Consultation, (published in *Friends World News*, No. 128, 1987, pp. 14-15), total world membership is 213,800, including 109,732 in North America. Although numbers in individual areas have varied from decade to decade, the totals have remained fairly constant. The big change is taking place in Third World countries, especially in Kenya, East Africa, which reached a membership of 45,000 in 1987. However, if the attenders were added in, it is likely that the count for Kenya would be 100,000 or more.

Africa	109,018
Asia and West Pacific	12,589
Europe and Near East	19,832
South America	34,020
Middle America	12,908
North America:	
Canada	1,130
United States	92,263
International and Miscellaneous	100
Total	**281,860**

Notes

INTRODUCTION

1. Howard Brinton, *Friends for 300 Years* (New York: Harper & Brothers, 1952), xiii-xiv.
2. Quoted from the student's paper.
3. The author is indebted in part to Dean Freiday for the concept of a "normative" view of Quakerism.
4. Quoted by Geoffrey F. Nuttall, *The Holy Spirit in Puritan Faith and Experience* (Oxford: Basil Blackwell, 1947), 24.

Chapter 1. A SHORT HISTORY

1. The main sources used here were Thomas D. Hamm, *The Transformation of American Quakerism: Orthodox Friends 1800-1907* (Bloomington: Indiana University Press, 1988), 36-143; Richard E. Wood, "The Rise of Semi-structured Worship and Paid Pastoral Leadership Among 'Gurneyite' Friends 1850-1900," in *Quaker Worship in North America*, ed. Francis B. Hall (Richmond, IN: Friends United Press, 1978), 53-74.
2. Hamm, *Transformation of American Quakerism*, 98.
3. Ibid., 125.
4. Mary S. Thomas, quoted in *Proceedings, Including Declaration of Christian Doctrine, General Conference of Friends, 1887*, 254.

Chapter 2. SOURCES OF RELIGIOUS AUTHORITY

1. With some editorial changes, this section draws heavily from my article, "Friends Understanding of the Light of Christ Within," *Quaker Life* (May 1982), 5-7.
2. George Fox, *Journal*, ed. Nickalls (Cambridge: The University Press, 1952), 406.
3. Robert Barclay, *Apology* (Philadelphia: Friends Book Store, 1908), 158.
4. Fox, *Journal*, 33.
5. Rachel Hadley King, *George Fox and the Light Within* (Philadelphia: Friends Book Store, 1940), 108.
6. Ibid., 98.
7. Howard Brinton, *The Religious Philosophy of Quakerism* (Wallingford, PA: Pendle Hill Publications, 1973), 27.
8. Barclay, *Apology*, 137, 141.
9. See Wilmer Cooper, "Is 'That of God in Everyone' the Touchstone of Quakerism?" *Quaker Life* (June 1981). Also see follow-up correspondence in *Quaker Life* (October and November 1981).
10. Barclay, *Apology*, 132.
11. Lewis Benson, *New Foundation: What Did George Fox Teach About Christ?* (Gloucester, England: George Fox Fund, 1976), 13.
12. Fox, *Journal*, 98.
13. An alternative interpretation is set forth by Elizabeth Isichei, *Victorian Quakers* (Oxford: Oxford University Press, 1970), 36. Writing about late nineteenth–century Friends, she says: "The Liberals claimed that any attempt to distinguish this Light from natural reason and conscience rendered the doctrine meaningless, and condemned Barclay, who made precisely this distinction, for dualism. All consciences are enlightened, though in different degrees, and conscience is always a spiritual faculty of man."
14. Barclay, *Apology*, 144.
15. Fox, *Journal*, 399-400.
16. Douglas Gwyn, "'Into That Which Cannot Be Shaken': The Apocalyptic Gospel Preached by George Fox," *The Day of the Lord*, ed. Dean Freiday (Newberg, OR: The Barclay Press, 1981), 87.
17. Richard K. Ullmann, *Friends and Truth* (London: Friends Home Service

Committee, 1955), 34.

18. Elbert Russell, *The Inner Light in the History and Present Problems of the Society of Friends* (Greensboro, NC: Friends Historical Society, 1945), 8.

19. Brinton, *Friends for 300 Years*, 40-41.

20. This statement appeared on the inside cover of the catalog of Earlham School of Religion in the early years of the school.

21. Material in this section has been drawn from my article on "Friends and the Holy Spirit," *Quaker Life* (October 1979), 5-9.

22. Fox, *Journal*, 40.

23. George H. Boobyer, *The Bible and the Light Within* (London: Friends Home Service Committee, 1973), 20.

24. Ibid., 20.

25. Ibid., 24.

26. Barclay, *Apology*, 72.

27. Fox, *Journal*, 145-6.

28. Barclay, *Apology*, 89.

29. Fox, *Journal*, 33.

30. Dorlan Bales, "Barclay's *Apology* in Context" (Ph.D. diss., University of Chicago, 1980), 283-285.

31. Barclay, *Apology*, 78.

32. Francis Frith, William Pollard, and William Edward Turner, "A Reasonable Faith," *Friends Quarterly* (October 1981): 353-404.

Chapter 3. QUAKER VIEW OF GOD

1. Rufus M. Jones, "The Quaker Conception of God," *Beyond Dilemmas: Quakers Look at Life*, ed. S. B. Laughlin (Philadelphia: J. B. Lippincott Company, 1937), 29.

2. Dean Freiday, *Nothing Without Christ* (Newberg, OR: The Barclay Press, 1984), 88.

3. Ibid., 87.

4. King, *Fox and the Light Within*, 169-70. King's conclusion that Fox did not believe in the bodily resurrection raises a question about her sources. Both Lewis Benson and Canby Jones, longtime students of Fox, conclude otherwise. Benson in his two-volume *Notes on George Fox* (Moorestown, NJ: Private publication, 1981), 1:118-119, has twenty-three entries from

Fox on the "Resurrection of Christ," most of which affirmed it. Canby Jones, from his study of Fox's *Epistles* says, "Though none of them [the *Epistles*] directly affirms that Fox believed in the 'bodily resurrection' he cites most of the scriptures used to support that view." For example, "He was crucified and buried, rose again the third day (I Cor. 15:4), ascended and is at the right hand of God" (Acts 2:32-34). Jones concludes: "The bodily resurrection ... is therefore strongly implied." See T. Canby Jones, *The Power of the Lord Is Over All: The Pastoral Letters of George Fox* (Richmond, IN: Friends United Press, 1989), Epistle 388, 419-20. Also see personal letter from Canby Jones, 21 July 1989.

5. Freiday, *Nothing Without Christ*, 87.
6. Ibid., 88 (for an essay on God by Samuel Fisher)
7. Margaret B. Hobling, "Early Friends and the Doctrine of the Trinity," *Then and Now*, ed. Anna Brinton (Philadelphia: University of Pennsylvania Press, 1960), 120.
8. Fox, *Journal*, 263.
9. Wilmer Cooper, "Is 'That of God in Everyone' The Touchstone of Quakerism?": *Quaker Life* (June 1981): 5-7; (October 1981): 23-24; (November 1981): 21-22.
10. H. G. Wood, *The Quaker Understanding of Christian Faith* (London: Friends Home Service Committee, 1955), 9.
11. Howard Brinton, *The Religious Philosophy of Quakerism* (Wallingford, PA: Pendle Hill Publications, 1973), 29.
12. Hugh Doncaster, *God in Every Man* (London: George Allen & Unwin Ltd., 1963), xiii.
13. Lewis Benson, "What Did Fox Mean by 'That of God in Every Man'"? *Quaker Religious Thought* (Spring 1970).
14. Daniel E. Bassuk, "Rufus Jones and Mysticism," *Quaker Religious Thought* (Summer 1978).
15. James F. Childress, "Answering That of God in Every Man," *Quaker Religious Thought* (Spring 1974).
16. Glenn Bartoo, *Decisions By Consensus* (Chicago: Progressive, 1978), 4.
17. From author's personal conversation with Rufus Jones on his deathbed.
18. Rufus M. Jones, *Friends Intelligencer* (17 July 1948), 105:408.
19. *Authorized Declaration of Faith of Five Years Meeting of Friends in America* (Richmond, IN: Friends United Press, n.d.), 11.
20. Fox, *Journal*, 602.

Chapter 4. QUAKER UNDERSTANDING OF CHRIST

1. Fox, *Journal*, 11.
2. King, *Fox and the Light Within*, 169.
3. It has long been acknowledged that "person" as used by the Greek Fathers (i.e., an actor's ability to represent more than one individual by wearing different masks) does not coincide with our contemporary understanding of personality or personhood.
4. The author is indebted to several sources for this section: Maurice A. Creasey, "Early Quaker Christology" (Ph.D. diss., University of Leeds, 1956); Maurice A. Creasey, "The Quaker Interpretation of the Significance of Christ," *Quaker Religious Thought*, vol. 1, no. 2 (Autumn 1959): 2-15; several of the writings of Lewis Benson, including "George Fox's Teaching About Christ," in "Christ as Prophet," *Quaker Religious Thought* vol. 16, nos. 1 and 2 (Winter 1974-75); John H. McCandless, *Quaker Understanding of Christ* (Philadelphia: Philadelphia Yearly Meeting, 1975); Hugh Barbour, "The Eyes That See: A Talk on a Quaker View of Jesus Christ" (Unpublished manuscript); Arthur 0. Roberts, "Early Friends and the Work of Christ," *Quaker Religious Thought*, vol. III, no, 1 (Spring 1961).
5. Creasey, *Quaker Christology*, 54.
6. Creasey, "Interpretation of the Significance of Christ," 3-4.
7. Ibid., 5.
8. Ibid., 8, quoted from Barclay's tract on *Universal Love*.
9. Ibid., 5.
10. Creasey, *Quaker Christology*, 68.
11. Ibid., 65-66.
12. Ibid., 74.
13. Ibid., 80.
14. Barclay, *Apology*, prop. V-VI, sect. XI, 132.
15. Ibid., prop. V-VI, sect. XV, 140.
16. Creasey, *Quaker Christology*, 94-95.
17. King, *Fox and the Light Within*, 165.
18. T. Canby Jones, "George Fox's Teaching on Redemption and Salvation" (Ph.D. diss., Yale University, 1955), 128.
19. Barclay, *Apology*, prop. 11, sect. V, 35.

20. Ibid., prop. V-VI, sect. XIII, 138.
21. King, *Fox and the Light Within*, 161-162.
22. Ibid., 163.
23. Ibid., 161-162. Rachel Hadley King points out that although for Fox "the cross within is little more than another synonym for the word or power within," nevertheless "this does not mean that he [Fox] does not believe that the historical Jesus died on a cross outside of Jerusalem."
24. Creasey, *Quaker Christology*, 111.
25. Ibid., 123.
26. Ibid., 125-126.
27. Benson, "Fox's Teaching About Christ," 21.
28. Ibid., 21.
29. Creasey, *Quaker Christology*, 127.
30. Ibid., 127-128.
31. Creasey, "Interpretation of the Significance of Christ," 9.
32. Benson, "Fox's Teaching About Christ," 26. The New Foundation Fellowship referred to follows closely the Lewis Benson attempt to recover the original vision of Quakerism *via* the life and work of George Fox.
33. Ibid., 27.
34. Ibid., 31-32.
35. Creasey, *Quaker Christology*, 136-137.
36. Rufus M. Jones, *The Later Periods of Quakerism* (London: Macmillan and Company, 1921), xvi-xvii.
37. A group calling themselves "Quaker Universalists" describe themselves in part as follows. "The 'QUG' is a group of people—mainly, but not exclusively, members of the Religious Society of Friends (Quakers) who see Quakerism as a spiritual path open to all, whatever the religious affiliation or lack of it .... Without wanting to promote an illusory search for a synthetic universal religion, or a broad common creed to which all people might subscribe, the QUG believes that all religious experience points toward a source of truth greater than that enshrined in any one religion."
38. Barclay, *Apology*, prop. V-VI, sect. XI. 132.
39. Ibid., prop. V-VI, sect. XXV, 180.
40. T. Canby Jones, ed., *Quaker Understanding of Christ and Authority* (Phila-

delphia: The Faith and Life Movement, Friends World Committee, American Section, 1974), 37-47.

41. Ibid., 43.

42. McCandless, *Quaker Understanding of Christ*, 15-16.

43. Ibid., 17.

44. Report of 1970 Faith and Life Conference, *What Future for Friends?* (Philadelphia: Friends World Committee, American Section, 1970), 39.

45. Arthur 0. Roberts, "Early Friends and the Work of Christ," *Quaker Religious Thought*, vol. III, no. 1 (Spring 1961), 10-20.

Chapter 5. QUAKER VIEW OF HUMAN NATURE

1. For a comprehensive treatment of the "Image of God" concept see David Cairns, *The Image of God in Man* (London: SCM Press, Ltd., 1953). This concept also relates to the Quaker principle of the Light of Christ Within (see 12-17), and the early Quaker doctrine of Christian perfection (see 64 -66).

2. Fox, *Journal*, 11.

3. George Fox, Sermon, 1680, 64. Quoted by T. Canby Jones, "George Fox's Teaching on Sin and Redemption" (Ph.D. diss., Yale University, 1955), 88.

4. Douglas Gwyn, "Captivity Among the Idols in Early Quakerism," *Quaker Religious Thought*, no. 66 (Fall 1987): 3-16.

5. Isaac Penington, *Works*, 4th ed., vol. 1 (Sherwood, N.Y.: David Heston, 1861), 167.

6. Ibid., 484.

7. Ibid.

8. Barclay, *Apology*, prop. IV, 97.

9. Ibid., prop. IV, sec. IV, 105-109.

10. Joseph John Gurney, *A Peculiar People: The Rediscovery of Primitive Christianity*, ed. Donald Green (Richmond, IN: Friends United Press, 1979), 4.

11. Ibid., 63.

12. *Journal of the Life and Religious Labours of Elias Hicks* (New York: Isaac T. Hopper, 1832), 259.

13. Ibid., 250.

14. *Letters of Elias Hicks, Including Also a Few Short Essays* (New York: Isaac T. Hopper, 1834), 53. For comparison of George Fox's view see ch. 4, 43, and 171, n. 23.

15. See Wilmer A. Cooper, "Rufus M. Jones and the Contemporary Quaker View of Man" (Ph.D. diss., Vanderbilt University, 1956); Wilmer A. Cooper, "Quaker Perspectives on the Nature of Man," *Quaker Religious Thought*, vol. II, no. 2 (Autumn 1960). Material in this chapter draws heavily from this article; in some cases the article is quoted directly with only minor changes.

16. Rufus M. Jones, "The Quaker Conception of God," *Beyond Dilemmas: Quakers Look at Life*, ed. S. B. Laughlin (Philadelphia: J. B. Lippincott Company, 1937), 40-41.

17. Rufus M. Jones, *The Double Search: Studies in Atonement and Prayer* (Philadelphia: The John C. Winston Company, 1906), 61.

18. Douglas Steere, *On Beginning From Within* (New York: Harper & Brothers, 1943), 104-105.

19. Ibid., 107.

20. D. Elton Trueblood, *Signs of Hope in a Century of Despair* (New York: Harper & Brothers, 1950), 56.

21. Ibid., 60.

22. Ibid., 65.

23. Arthur O. Roberts, *The People Called Quakers* (Newberg, OR: Oregon Yearly Meeting, ca. 1955), 12.

24. Cecil E. Hinshaw, *Toward Political Responsibility* (Wallingford, PA.: Pendle Hill, 1954), 21-22.

25. The Third World Conference of Friends, *Friends Face Their Fourth Century* (London: Friends World Committee for Consultation, 1952), xviii.

26. Kenneth E. Boulding, *The Organizational Revolution: A Study in The Ethics of Economic Organization* (New York: Harper & Brothers, 1953), 78.

27. Douglas Steere, *On Beginning*, xi.

28. Fox, *Journal*, 52, 56.

29. Ibid., 27.

30. Penington, *Works*, vol. IV, 239.

31. Barclay, *Apology*, prop. VIII, 234.

32. Ibid., 234-235.
33. The author has personally heard Tillich thus define salvation.
34. Dean Freiday, *Barclay's Apology in Modem English* (2 Garfield Terrace, Elberon, NJ.: Published privately, 1967), 254, n. 19.
35. Fox, *Journal*, 65. Fox's statement referred to his testimony against war and fighting, but he applied the same principle to other areas of life.
36. Ibid., 34.
37. Freiday, *Barclay's Apology*, 72.
38. Gurney, *A Peculiar People*, 59-60,

Chapter 6. QUAKER UNDERSTANDING OF THE CHURCH

1. See Brinton, *Friends for 300 Years*, x, for discussion of this. Also, see Lewis Benson, *Catholic Quakerism* (Philadelphia: Book Service Committee, Philadelphia Yearly Meeting, 1966), ch. 1, which sets forth his view.
2. Brinton., *Friends for 300 Years*, 59. (For another reference to this kind of typology see Maurice Creasey, " Worship in the Christian Tradition," in *Quaker Worship in North America*, ed. Francis B. Hall (Richmond, IN: Friends United Press, 1978), 1.
3. See Ernst Troeltsch, *The Social Teachings of the Christian Churches*, trans. Olive Wyon, 2 vols, (London: Allen & Unwin, 1931).
4. John Timothy Terrell, "The Movement from Sect to Denomination in Nineteenth–Century Gurneyite Quakerism," M.A. Thesis (Richmond, IN: Earlham School of Religion, 1985).
5. The author is indebted to Charles F. Thomas for the formulation of these characteristics, with some editorial additions and revisions added. The author co-taught a Quakerism course with Charles Thomas where these points were presented in fuller form.
6. Charles F. Thomas, "On Being a People of God," *The Church in Quaker Thought and Practice*, ed. Charles F. Thomas (Richmond, IN: Faith and Life Movement *via* Friends World Committee, 1979), 27-36.
7. Donald Nesti, C.S.Sp., *Grace and Faith: The Means of Salvation* (Pittsburgh: Catholic Quaker Studies, No. 3, 1975), 207-307.
8. Donald Nesti, C.S.Sp., "The Early Quaker Ecclesiology," *Quaker Religious Thought*, vol. 18, no. 1 (Autumn 1978): 8
9. Gladys Wilson, *Quaker Worship* (London; Banisdale Press, 1952), 76.

10. T. Canby Jones, ed., "*The Power of the Lord Is Over All*," Epistle 288, 283-284.
11. Ibid., Epistle 33, 25-26.
12. Ibid.
13. Wilson, *Quaker Worship*, 41.
14. Barclay, *Apology*, prop. XI, 340.
15. John Griffith quoted by Lucia K. Beamish, *Quaker Ministry 1691-1834* (Oxford, England: Printed privately, 1967), 64.
16. Ibid., 63.
17. Ibid., 65-80.
18. A. Neave Brayshaw, *The Quakers: Their Story and Message* (London: Friends Home Service Committee, 1921), 251.
19. For a treatment of Quaker Quietism see Elbert Russell, *History of Quakerism* (New York: Macmillan Company, 1943), ch. 18.
20. See Wilmer A. Cooper, *The ESR Story: A Quaker Dream Come True* (Richmond, IN: Earlham School of Religion, 1985), especially ch. 1, 1-10, for background efforts on training for pastoral ministry.
21. Again the author is indebted to Charles Thomas and D. Elton Trueblood for the early formulation of these points. The author co-taught a Quakerism course with Charles Thomas where these points were more fully spelled out.
22. This was first given as the Quaker Lecture at Indiana Yearly Meeting in 1960, and subsequently published in *Quaker Religious Thought*, vol. iv, no. 2 (Autumn 1962).
23. Lewis Benson, "The People of God and Gospel Order," *The Church in Quaker Thought and Practice*, ed. Charles F. Thomas (Richmond, IN: Quakers Faith and Life Movement *via* Friends World Committee, 1979), 19.

Chapter 7. FRIENDS AND THE SACRAMENTS

1. Alan Kolp, "Friends, Sacraments and the Future," *Friends and the Sacraments* (Richmond, IN: Friends United Press, 1981), 10-13.
2. Elfrida Vipont Foulds elaborates on this Quaker phrase in her pamphlet, *Let Your Lives Speak* (London: Friends Home Service Committee, 1953).

3. Most of this chapter is taken from the author's contribution to "*Friends and the Sacraments*," 3-9.

4. Those who believe that baptism and the Lord's Supper were ordained by Jesus have used the term "ordinances" instead of "sacraments," the latter not being a biblical term.

5. Maurice Creasey, "Quakers and the Sacraments," *Quaker Religious Thought* (Spring 1963): 19, 22.

6. Ibid., 10.

7. The question has been raised whether Fox and early Friends were anti-Semitic, or whether their denunciation of the old Jewish covenant simply represented the Quaker understanding of how God was revealed in human history.

8. Henry Cadbury in *The Nature of the Church*, ed. R. Newton Flew (New York: Harper & Brothers, 1952), 306.

9. Creasey, "Quakers and the Sacraments," 10.

10. See also Mark 1:8; Luke 3:16; John 1:33; Acts 1:5; 11:16.

11. Canby Jones, "George Fox and the Interpretation of the Sacraments" (Private paper), 1, 4, 7.

12. Rufus M. Jones, *The Society of Friends and the Sacraments* (London, Friends Book Centre, 1935), 6.

13. See the work on the "Western Text" by Wescott and Hort, 1881.

14. Edward Grubb, *The Last Supper* (London: Friends Home Service Committee, 1930), 7.

15. Gerald K. Hibbert, *Friends and the Sacraments* (London: Friends Home Service Committee, 1944), 11-12.

16. D. Elton Trueblood, *The People Called Quakers* (New York: Harper and Row, 1966), 138.

17. *Christian Faith and Practice* (London: London Yearly Meeting, 1960), No. 214.

18. Dean Freiday, "The Biblical Evidence for the Sacraments: A Critical Examination" (private paper) 6, 20, 26. Freiday says there is no systematic treatment of sacraments until Thomas Aquinas's *Summa* in the thirteenth century. Also the claim that sacraments convey grace for salvation came with the Council of Trent in the sixteenth century.

19. This is the title of a World Council of Churches document that has been under study for a number of years by the member churches.

20. For an insightful discussion of this from a Quaker perspective see Jay W. Marshall, "'Eucharistic Fellowship'—Are Friends Included?" *Quaker Religious Thought*, #70 (Winter 1988-89): 28-37.
21. *Friends and the Sacraments* (Richmond, IN: Friends United Press, 1981), 2.

Chapter 8. THE QUAKER TESTIMONIES

1. William Penn, *No Cross, No Crown* (Philadelphia: T. K. & P. G. Collins, 1853), 85.
2. Ibid., 62.
3. Ibid., 204.
4. See Jones, *"The Power of the Lord Is Over All,"* 223-234 passim.
5. Freiday, *Barclay's Apology*, 389.
6. Worth Hartman (term paper, Earlham School of Religion, 1984).
7. *Christian Faith and Practice* (London: London Yearly Meeting, 1960), no. 660.
8. For a brief treatment of Quaker philanthropy see Elbert Russell, *History of Quakerism* (New York: The MacMillan Co., 1943), 251-268.
9. Cecil Hinshaw, "Christian Perfection in Quakerism" (Quaker Lecture, Earlham School of Religion, 1974), 4. Also see Cecil Hinshaw, *An Apology for Perfection,* Pendle Hill Pamphlet No. 138 (Wallingford, PA: Pendle Hill, 1964).
10. Fox, *Journal*, 3.
11. Hinshaw, "Christian Perfection in Quakerism," 3.
12. Dietrich Bonhoeffer, *Cost of Discipleship* (London: SCM Press, 1937). Chapter 11 on "Truth-telling" has an excellent treatment of this subject that very much reflects the Quaker point of view.
13. Phillips Moulton, ed., "A Plea for the Poor," *Journal and Major Essays of John Woolman* (New York: Oxford University Press, 1971), 241.
14. *Christian Faith and Practice*, (London) no. 614.
15. See previous discussion of "That of God in Everyone", 29-31.
16. Hinshaw, "Christian Perfection in Quakerism," 8.
17. Fox, *Journal*, 65.
18. Howard Brinton, *The Peace Testimony of The Society of Friends* (Philadelphia: American Friends Service Committee, 1951), 4 (out of print).

19. London *Christian Faith and Practice*, no. 395.
20. Benjamin Seaver, "Three Definitions of Peace," reprinted from *The Friend* (Philadelphia: 17 April 1952).
21. Howard Brinton, *Guide to Quaker Practice*, Pendle Hill Pamphlet No. 20 (Wallingford, PA: Pendle Hill, 1955). See his discussion of the Quaker testimonies, 55-64.
22. Frederick B. Tolles, "Quakerism and Politics," *Quakers and the Atlantic Culture* (New York: Macmillan Co., 1960), 36-54.
23. Ibid., 39-40.

Chapter 9. LAST THINGS AND ETERNAL HOPE

1. Howard Brinton, *Religious Philosophy of Quakerism*, 32.
2. Gwyn, "'Into That Which Cannot Be Shaken'"; also see Douglas Gwyn, *Apocalypse of the Word* (Richmond, IN: Friends United Press, 1986).
3. Gwyn, "Into That Which Cannot Be Shaken," 70.
4. Ibid., 73.
5. T. Canby Jones, "George Fox's Understanding of Last Things," *Friends Quarterly* (October 1954): 204.
6. See fuller discussion of the Offices of Christ in chapter 4.
7. These two positions can be further studied by looking at Thomas G. Sanders, *Protestant Concepts of Church and State* (New York, Doubleday & Company, 1964), 137, 142; Tolles, *Quakers and the Atlantic Culture*, ch. 3. In the latter, Tolles describes the absolutist and relativist positions, which loosely correspond with those Friends who reject working through the institutions of government and those who advocate doing so in order to realize the will of God. The absolutist/Gospel Order position is reflected in the writings of Lewis Benson, e.g., his *Catholic Quakerism* (Philadelphia, PA: Philadelphia Yearly Meeting, 1966). This position has also been stated by Douglas Gwyn's chapter "Into That Which Cannot Be Shaken," especially 69, 86-87.
8. Fox, *Journal*, 19.
9. Parker Palmer, "Born Again: The Monastic Way to Church Renewal," *Weavings*, vol. I. no. 1 (September/October 1986), l6.
10. E. Herman, *Creative Prayer* (New York: Harper & Brothers, n.d.).
11. Charles Whiston was an Episcopal priest and professor who conducted

prayer workshops for seminarians for many years.

12. Kenneth Boulding, *There Is a Spirit: The Nayler Sonnets* (New York: Fellowship Publications, 1945), x.

Chapter 10. QUAKER MISSION, SERVICE, AND OUTREACH

1. Stated in an address to The National Conference of United Society of Friends Women, High Point, NC, 1959.

2. The facts and figures given here and following are taken from Wilmer A. Cooper, "The Ethical Implications of Quakers in Politics" (unpublished M.A. thesis, Haverford College, 1948).

3. Tolles, *Quakers and the Atlantic Culture* , 50-51.

4. Cooper, "Ethical Implications," 26-28.

5. Tolles, *Quakers and The Atantic Culture*, 44. After the 1722 Act of Affirmation Quakers were allowed to substitute an affirmation for an oath, except for the oath required for public office. The latter was not instituted until after the Reform Act of 1832.

6. Ibid., 53-54.

7. For fuller treatment of these subjects see Paul Herman Emden, *Quakers and Commerce* (London: Sampson Low, 1939), and Arthur Raistrick, *Quakers in Science and Industry* (London: Bannisdale Press, 1950).

8. Kenneth Boulding, *The Prospering of Truth*, Swarthmore Lecture (London: Friends Home Service Committee, 1970), 42.

9. Hugh Barbour, "A Short History of Quaker Service," *Consultation on Quaker Service* (Richmond, IN: Quaker Hill Conference Center and Earlham School of Religion, 1980), 1-2.

10. Brayshaw, *The Quakers: Their Story and Message*, n., 303.

11. Ibid., 303-304.

12. Ibid., 305. Although Richardson's reference to "heathen nations" may seem harsh, his main point—that settled communities of faith require more than casual visits by traveling Friends—is valid.

13. Harold Smuck, Lecture on Friends Missions; Earlham School of Religion, May 1975.

14. A good brief account of Friends foreign mission work can be found in Elbert Russell, *History of Quakerism*, 435-448. A fuller account is given by Henry T. Hodgkin, *Friends Beyond the Seas* (London: Headley Brothers,

1916); Levinus K. Painter, *The Hill of Vision*, (Kaimosi, Kenya: East Africa Yearly Meeting, 1951); and Harold Smuck, *Friends in East Africa* (Richmond, IN: Friends United Press, 1987).

15. A. Ruth Fry, *A Quaker Adventure: The Story of Nine Years Relief and Reconstruction* (London: Nisbet, 1926), 1-2.

16. For an overview of the work of the American Friends Service Committee in its earlier years see Rufus M. Jones, *A Service of Love in War Time: American Friends Relief Work in Europe 1917-19* (New York: The Macmillan Company, 1920), and Clarence E. Pickett, *For More Than Bread* (Boston: Little, Brown, 1953), *Witness For Humanity* (Wallingford, PA: Pendle Hill, 1999).

17. For a survey of Quakers in education, see Howard Brinton, *Quaker Education in Theory and Practice* (Wallingford, PA: Pendle Hill, 1949); Helen G. Hole, *Things Civil and Useful: A Personal View of Quaker Education* (1978); and Elbert Russell, *History of Quakerism*, chs. 13 and 33.

18. Russell, *History of Quakerism*, 156.

19. Ibid., 161.

20. For a summary of Quaker influence on education in the nineteenth century, see Russell, *History of Quakerism*, 449-461.

21. See list of Quaker schools in Hole, *Things Civil and Useful*, 133-134.

Chapter 11. QUAKER ASSESSMENT AND FUTURE PROSPECTS

1. Rufus M. Jones, *Original Quakerism-A Movement, Not A Sect* (Richmond, IN: Five Years Meeting, 1945), 3.

2. Ibid., 2. Jones's definition of "sect" differs somewhat from the classical formulations of Max Weber, Ernst Troeltsch, and Richard Niebuhr. Niebuhr, for example, defines a sect as a voluntary organization requiring a particular religious experience; emphasis on the priesthood of all believers while de-emphasizing official clergy; strong Christian ethical concern that emphasizes separation from the world rather than compromise; and the sect often represents the minority. See H. Richard Niebuhr, *The Social Sources of Denominationalism* (New York: Meridian Books, Inc., 1957), 17-21.

3. John Timothy Terrell, "The Movement from Sect to Denomination in

Nineteenth Century Gurneyite Quakerism" (M.A. thesis, Earlham School of Religion, 1985). Terrell's definition of sect, contrary to that given by Rufus Jones, follows the classical definition of sect spelled out in the previous footnote.

4. Ibid., 3.
5. Benson, *Catholic Quakerism*, 11.
6. Jones, *Original Quakerism*, 20.
7. Ibid., 24.
8. "Membership Statistics of the Religious Society of Friends 1937-1987," *Friends World News*, no. 128 (1987): 14-15. Also see Appendix B, 166.
9. For statistics used here see Gordon M, Browne, Jr., *The Future of Quakerism* (Philadelphia: Wider Quaker Fellowship, 1987), 8-9.
10. For an important analysis of this see Jack D. Marietta, *The Reformation of American Quakerism 1748-1783* (Philadelphia: University of Pennsylvania Press, 1984), 3-31.
11. For a comprehensive treatment of the 1887 Richmond Conference see Mark Minear, *Richmond 1887: A Quaker Drama Unfolds* (Richmond, IN: Friends United Press, 1987).
12. For a treatment of the Manchester Conference and the liberal movement surrounding it, see special issue of *Friends Quarterly*, entitled "A Reasonable Faith" (October 1984).
13. Wilmer Cooper, *The Gospel According To Friends* (Richmond, IN: Friends United Press, 1986), 12. For further discussion of "normative" Quakerism see 11-13, Also see "Introduction" by Wilmer Cooper in *Quaker Understanding of Christ and Authority*, ed. T. Canby Jones (Philadelphia: The Faith and Life Movement and distributed by Friends World Committee, American Section, 1974), 7-9, and 12, n. 2.
14. Address by Hugh Doncaster to 1967 Friends World Conference at Guilford College, NC, *Quaker Life* (September 1967): 295.
15. Everett Cattell, "The Future of Friends," *Quaker Religious Thought*, vol. VIII, no. 2 (Autumn 1966): 10-14, and Everett L. Cattell, "A New Approach For Friends," *What Future For Friends?* (Philadelphia: Friends World Committee, American Section 1970), 32-44.
16. Cattell, "A New Approach For Friends," 35.
17. Ibid., 34-35.
18. Cattell, "The Future of Friends," 12.

19. Cattell, "A New Approach For Friends," 39.

20. Maurice A. Creasey, "A Frame of Reference for Friends," *Quaker Religious Thought*, vol. VIII, no. 2 (Autumn 1966): 18.

21. Maurice A. Creasey and Harold Loukes, *The Next 50 Years* (London: Friends Home Service Committee, 1956), 14.

22. Ibid.

23. A formidable analysis of the Universalist/Christian debate among Friends is set forth by Barbara Olmsted in "Can Friends Be Both Universalist-Minded and Christ-Centered?" *Friends Journal* (November 1988), 8-10, The author has cited excellent passages from Robert Barclay and John Woolman to confirm both the universalist and Christian basis for historical Quakerism, but her final disavowal of Christ-centered language seems inconsistent with her basic argument.

24. Address by Seth Hinshaw to National Conference of United Society of Friends Women, High Point, NC, 1959.

25. Cattell, "The Future of Friends," 14.

26. Leonard Kenworthy, *The Religious Society of Friends: Our Mission and Our Message-Bearers* (Kennett Square, PA: Quaker Publications, 1984), 4.

27. Cooper, *The Gospel According to Friends*, 14. This faith and hope formula is drawn from the experience of the World Council of Churches to which the author served as Quaker representative on the Faith and Order Commission in 1968-1975.

Glossary

Agnosticism—Expression of doubt or skepticism about our ability to have knowledge of God or of any ultimate truth, resulting in skepticism about religious faith as such.

Anabaptists—The religious tradition of the Mennonites and Church of the Brethren originating in Switzerland in the sixteenth century. They advocated adult baptism in place of infant baptism and aimed to be followers of Jesus by living out the Sermon on the Mount.

Antinomianism—Freedom from, or disregard for, obligation to the moral law. It claims salvation by grace unencumbered by any moral constraints.

Apocalyptic—Usually refers to biblical writings (such as the book of Daniel and the book of Revelation) that use veiled language and symbols to disclose prophetic warnings, hopes, and aspirations in bad times or in the face of end time.

Apollinarianism—Fourth century attempt to define the relationship of the divine and human in Jesus Christ by asserting that he was human in his fleshly body and nature, while his human rational mind was replaced by Christ's divine mind—the incarnate Logos of God. Thus the center of personality for Jesus Christ was divine rather than human.

Arminianism—A doctrine of free will allowing human beings to respond to the free grace of God. This was proclaimed by Jacobus Arminius (1560-1609) to counter Calvin's doctrine of election and predestination.

Atonement—The reconciliation and restoration of broken relationships, especially between human beings and God. In Hebrew thought, the sacrifice of animals (involving the shedding of blood) was regarded as instrumental in effecting atonement. Thus in Christian theology Jesus Christ represents the supreme sacrifice needed to effect reconciliation between God and humans. Atonement has to do with the saving work of Christ.

Attenders—Persons who attend and participate in the life of Friends meetings without becoming members.

Calvinism—The Reformed tradition among sixteenth–century Protestants who followed the doctrines and practices of John Calvin of Geneva (1509-1564). Although George Fox preached a message very much at odds with Calvinistic doctrine, the Calvinist Puritan milieu out of which Quakerism came influenced Quaker thought and practice in significant ways. (See also **Puritans**.)

Charismatic—Usually refers to a spirit of Pentecostalism and spiritual enthusiasm within Christian congregations. The word derives from two Greek words: *charis* (grace, gift, or power) and *pneuma* (spirit, breath, or wind).

Christology—Theological reasoning and reflection about the person and work of Jesus Christ as the central revelation of God in history.

Demonic—In a religious context this refers to possession by evil forces and spirits, often personified by Satan or the Devil.

Dissenters—Protestant communicants in the seventeenth century who refused to conform to the Church of England. Prior to the Restoration under Charles II they were usually called Nonconformists. Quakers were classified among them. (See also Nonconformists.)

Docestism—A third–century church teaching which emphasized the divinity of Jesus Christ at the expense of his humanity, namely, the view that his humanity and suffering only "seemed" to be real.

Ecclesiology—The theology of church government, structure, and organization.

Election—Doctrine proclaimed by John Calvin that God elects (chooses) those who will experience salvation. It may also refer to the elect (or chosen) people of God e.g., Israel. (See also Predestination.)

Eschatology—Theology of "last things" or "end time" in the context of which one measures the promise of eternal hope. The term "realized eschatology" is a modern concept that recognizes the possibility of spiritual fulfillment and entrance into the kingdom of God here and now rather than at the end of history. In the Quaker tradition it means responding to "the Day of Visitation" and living a life of holy obedience here and now in this world.

Evangelical—Evangelical Friends emphasize Orthodox Christian doctrine based on the authority of the Bible. They point to Jesus Christ as the unique revelation of God and hold that Jesus died on the cross to atone for human sin and rose again from the dead to triumph over evil. The Holy Spirit is the means of God's immediate revelation for the purpose of discerning and applying biblical truth. Evangelicals respond to the Great Commission in Matthew 28 to "go and make disciples of all nations." They are largely, though not solely, identified with the pastoral/programmed meetings in the Gurney Orthodox tradition of Friends.

Eucharist—Celebration of the Lord's Supper or Holy Communion.

Evil—In the broad sense evil refers to all that is "not good" in the world. Historically, evil has had a dual meaning: moral evil , which breaks the moral law, is personal, and is that for which we are responsible. Natural evil, on the other hand, includes all that runs counter to the good and for which human beings are not directly responsible. This includes natural disasters, famines, floods, tornadoes, disease, poverty, war, human suffering, and death. While humanity may be indirectly responsible for some of these, others are legally called "acts of God."

Fall—Genesis 1-3 describes the fall of Adam and Eve from a state of innocence and perfection into a condition of sin and alienation from the Creator. This constitutes a parable about the sinful condition of the human race caused by the disobedience of Adam and Eve in the Garden of Eden.

Forensic—A legal act of God to restore divine justice in relationship to the human betrayal of God's will in the Fall.

Free Church—The dissenting churches, especially in England in the seventeenth century, which broke away from the established state churches, such as the Church of England. Membership was voluntary and adult baptism was practiced.

Gospel Order—A term used by George Fox to describe the new covenant order of the church under the headship of Christ. It assumes the presence of Christ among the people of God to give direction to those who would be obedient followers. Fox's objective was to restore God's order of creation before the Fall.

Gnosticism—A first century teaching in the early church which claimed true knowledge (*gnosis*) of the higher truths and mysteries of religion. It denied the goodness of creation, the reality of bodily life, and the humanity of Jesus. It over-spiritualized the real world.

High Church—See **Liturgical** and **Low Church**.

Imago Dei—The Genesis claim that man and woman were created in the image of God; that in spite of the Fall human beings retain and reflect certain divine qualities, such as creativity, rationality, and the moral sense of right and wrong.

Immanence—God (or the Divine) is inherent in human experience and continues to act within the created world and in history. Immanence is the opposite pole of transcendence in terms of God's relationship to the world. The Hebrew-Christian tradition of the Bible proclaims that Deity is both transcendent and immanent, perhaps best expressed in the Christian doctrine of the Incarnation.

Immortality—The Greek idea that at death the soul of a human being sloughs off its physical embodiment and goes back to God—into a state of eternal existence. The Greek doctrine of immortality stands in contrast to the biblical view of the resurrection of the body as a whole being uniting spirit and nature.

Incarnation—The belief of Christians that God was revealed in the person of Jesus Christ within historical time. The Incarnation (as compared with the Hebrew messianic idea) was the Greek way of expressing Jesus Christ's unique personification of both the humanity and the divinity of the Godhead.

Justification—Reconciliation with God by means of which God forgives and accepts the sinner who has been disobedient. It also means the restoration of a right relationship between God the Creator and persons who have been created by God.

Koinonia—The New Testament term applied to the early Christian community, usually translated "fellowship." It constitutes a community or fellowship of persons unified by agape love.

Liberal—Liberal Friends hold that belief must be verified by religious experience. They acknowledge the authority of the biblical revelation within the context of historical/critical study. Religious experience derives from the direct revelation of God through the Light of Christ within. Through the Light within we can not only know the truth but we can be empowered to "do the truth." Liberals emphasize the life, teachings and death of Jesus as our example for the way of love in the world. They have been concerned to reconcile science and religion, and to incorporate freedom of thought, tolerance and humanitarian service in the expression of religious faith and practice. Friends try to maintain a balance between individual liberty and the corporate discipline of the group, the Friends meeting.

Liturgical—A form of worship that employs liturgy, creeds, ritual, and sacraments. It represents the more formal and structured "high church" type of Christian worship, ministry, and congregational organization.

Logos—The Greek name given to the pre-existent Christ in the prologue to the gospel of John. Logos referred to the eternal principle, wisdom, reason, and Word of God. It was believed that the Logos was generated out of the substance of God rather than created by God.

Low Church—The non-liturgical Free Church tradition that places a premium on the freedom of the Spirit in worship, ministry, and congregational organization. It contrasts with the more formal and structured worship and church life of the liturgical and sacramental churches (e.g., Roman Catholic and Episcopalian).

Manichaeism—A third century, Persian based, form of dualistic thought similar to Gnosticism. It regarded humans to be in bondage to the material realm of evil while seeking escape to the realm of the Light.

Nonconformist—Religious dissenters (mainly Puritan), especially prior to the Restoration of Charles II in 1660. After the Restoration they were usually referred to as Dissenters, including the Quakers. (See also Dissenters.)

Normative—This term refers to an ethical norm, standard or practice, such as the testimonies of the Religious Society of Friends. As used in this book it also means that certain standards of behavior and certain testimonies express Quaker social concern and that these standards have been objectively adhered to and practiced throughout Quaker history. In this manner these standards, such as the Peace Testimony, have become normative for Friends.

Pelagianism—The teaching of the English monk Pelagius (c. 383-409/10) who advocated a doctrine of free will instead of the more deterministic and predestinarian doctrines of Augustine (354-430). Pelagius's doctrine of free will ran counter to the doctrine of original sin. He regarded the will as free to choose good or evil. Because he claimed persons can save themselves without being dependent upon the grace of God, Pelagius was attacked by Augustine.

Predestination—A doctrine that holds that all that happens in the world from all eternity is foreordained by God. This led to the accompanying doctrine of election held by Augustine in the fourth and fifth centuries and by John Calvin in the sixteenth century. Double predestination maintains that God elects some to salvation and others to damnation. The Arminians (followers of Jacobus Arminius [1560-1609]) at the end of the sixteenth century and the Quakers in the seventeenth century rejected outright the doctrines of predestination and election in favor of the free accountability of every adult person before God.

Puritans—Those in the Calvinist (Presbyterian) tradition in sixteenth and seventeenth– century England who set out to purify the Church of England. They were among the Nonconformists and Dissenters in the seventeenth century who represented left-wing Protestantism. It was primarily out of this "fag end of the Protestant Reformation" (as one English historian described the Quakers) that the followers of George Fox came to form the Religious Society of Friends. (See also Calvinism.)

Ranterism—A seventeenth–century movement of religious individualism, radicalism, antinomianism, and anarchy that claimed to have a corner on the truth as revealed to individual persons. They relied on the Inward Light devoid of any outward checks or restraints. There was some crossing over between the Ranters and the Quakers in the seventeenth century.

Realized Eschatology—(See Eschatology.)

Redemption—The restoration of one's right relationship with God following separation through sin and disobedience. In Christian thought redemption involves the same process as salvation, atonement, and justification. In Christian history redemption implied the payment of ransom in order to assure deliverance from evil. It is God who redeems and restores a right relationship between God and the sinner, and in Christian faith this is accomplished through the Redeemer (mediator) Jesus Christ. The result is newness of life and a restored relationship with God and fellow human beings.

Reprobation—Rejection by God. In the tradition of predestinarianism it means that rejection by God was foreordained.

Resurrection—The early church was founded on the conviction that God had raised Jesus from the dead after the Crucifixion and that the resurrected Christ had won a victory over the demonic forces of sin and death. Thus the Resurrection, however one may understand its details, vindicated the sovereignty and power of God to overcome evil. In another sense the resurrection of the body (the soma) may be compared with the immortality of the soul in the Greek tradition. Hebrew thought understood the body to be a whole person with no distinction between soul and body. The resurrection faith was that the whole body (or person) is resurrected from the dead—not just the indestructible soul as claimed by the Greeks. Resurrection is also seen as a spiritual event in the life of the Christian believer—namely, as one is baptized by the Spirit in the community of faith one is raised in newness of life in the kingdom of God. Thus by faith one participates in the resurrected body of Christ here and now.

Sacramental—Friends regard all life as potentially sacramental—namely, every event can become an occasion for the presence of God. All of life (e.g., every meal) can be an outward sign of the inward grace and transforming power of God. Indeed, our physical and visible lives should at all times serve as outward expressions and manifestations of the inward life of the Spirit.

Salvation —Because of our sin we are separated and alienated from God. Salvation means overcoming that separation and alienation by being reconciled and reunited with God as the spiritual ground of our being. The Latin root for salvation is *salvus*, which can be translated "health" or "wholeness"; thus salvation means a relationship with God and our fellow humans that is spiritually healthy and whole.

Sanctification—Following repentance and conversion to the Christian life, sanctification means growth toward maturity in the life of the Spirit. In those traditions that espouse Christian perfection as a goal, sanctification means to be made holy; in the Quaker view it means to attain a life of Christian perfection where we are enabled to live up to the measure of the Light given us. In the Wesleyan tradition it means a second work of grace (beyond conversion) is necessary to bring one into a state of Christian perfection.

Savior—In a Christian context this refers specifically to Jesus Christ as the Savior of humankind and the world. As a theological concept, however, humanity's need for a savior recognizes that we cannot save ourselves but are ultimately dependent upon the grace, mercy, and love of God for salvation.

Sectarian—Often this term has a negative connotation, implying a narrow and bigoted point of view. In the context of church history it is applied to those church groups or sects that have separated from the mainline churches and denominations. Again, the implication is negative—namely, separation from the mainstream of Christendom. Quakers and those in the Anabaptist tradition (Mennonites and Brethren) often have been regarded as sectarian. They de-emphasize the role of clergy and the use of liturgy in worship; they emphasize ethical concern guided by the Sermon on the Mount, separation from the world's ways in order not to compromise with principle, the priesthood of all believers, and voluntary membership and baptism at the age of accountability.

Sin—In the biblical and Christian traditions sin is the name given to moral evil. In this context it means defiance of God's will in favor of self-will. Sin is the temptation (ascribed to original sin) to choose evil rather than the good; to choose self-will rather than God's will. Sin is against God, the one who created us and to whom we are accountable. Thus sin is not against an abstract moral law. In the Quaker tradition sin is defiance of the truth, or "being out of the truth," as opposed to "doing the truth." Sins (the plural) are acts of disobedience against the will of God.

Soul—In Greek thought, the soul represents the divine, indestructible, and immortal dimension of human beings. In Christian thought, it is the seat of reason and will of personhood, created by God, and it overcomes death. In modern psychological and existential thought the focus is not on the soul but on the self as the center of personhood.

Testimonies—Friends testimonies are an outward expression of inward spiritual leadings and discernments of truth and the will of God. They constitute the moral and ethical fruit of the inward life of the Spirit. See Chapter 11 for a distinction between the Religious and Social Testimonies of Friends.

Transcendence—The Hebrew-Christian tradition of the Bible proclaims that the Deity is both transcendent and immanent, perhaps best expressed in the

Christian doctrine of the Incarnation. God (or the Divine) stands above, beyond, and apart from the created world order. Transcendence is the opposite pole of immanence in terms of God's relationship to the world.

Trinity—Sometimes referred to as the Triunity of God. In Christian doctrine it involves the focus of unity and diversity of the Godhead in terms of God the Father, Christ the Son, and the Holy Spirit. In the early church there was much preoccupation with the metaphysical nature of the persons of the Trinity. The struggle was to preserve the unity of the Godhead without denying the legitimate role of the three persons. It also attempted to define the relationship of the divine and human in the Godhead. Quakers were always concerned to maintain the spiritual unity of God, Christ, and Holy Spirit. They were only interested in the Trinity as a functional or experiential concept—namely, that devotion to God also implies an experiential relationship with the inward Christ and with Christ's continuing Holy Spirit. Although they spurned Trinitarian theology, Friends were concerned to maintain the unity of the Godhead.

Vehiculum Dei—A term employed by Robert Barclay in his Apology to describe the divine principle, light or seed in which God dwells in each person. Vehiculum Dei literally means "divine conveyor," by means of which God and Christ are made available and are subject to being received and accepted in the human heart.

Wesleyanism—The influence of evangelical Methodism, which impacted Quakerism in England and America in the nineteenth century.

Select Bibliography

Very little of book length has been written systematically on the theological beliefs of Friends. Many tracts and pamphlets have been produced, but they are too numerous to list here. The following books, which are both historical and theological in nature, will be useful to the general reader and will provide helpful interpretive background information on Quaker beliefs.

A Brief Synopsis of the Principles and Testimonies of the Religious Society of Friends. Joint publication of Conservative Yearly Meetings, 1913.

Barbour, Hugh, and J. William Frost. *The Quakers.* New York: Greenwood Press, 1988.

Barclay, Robert. *Barclay's Apology in Modern English.* Edited by Dean Freiday. Elberon, N. J.: private printing, 1967.

Benson, Lewis. *Catholic Quakerism.* 4th printing. Philadelphia: Book Service Committee of Philadelphia Yearly Meeting, 1983.

Brinton, Howard. *Friends for 300 Years.* Wallingford, PA: Pendle Hill Publication, 1964.

_____. *Guide to Quaker Practice.* Pamphlet No. 20. Wallingford, PA: Pendle Hill Publication, 1955.

_____. *The Religious Philosophy of Quakerism.* Wallingford, PA: Pendle Hill Publication, 1973.

Creasey, Maurice A. *Bearings: Friends and the New Reformation.* Swarthmore Lecture 1969. London: Friends Home Service Committee, 1969.

Fox, George. *Journal.* Edited by Rufus M. Jones, with glossary by Howard Alexander. Richmond, IN: Friends United Press, 1976.

Freiday, Dean. *Nothing Without Christ: Some Current Problems in Religious Thought in the Light of Seventeenth Century Thought and Experience.* Newberg, OR: The Barclay Press, 1984.

Gurney, Joseph John. *A Peculiar People: The Rediscovery of Primitive Christianity.* Edited by Donald Green. Richmond, IN: Friends United Press, 1979.

Gwyn, Douglas. *Apocalypse of the Word: The Life and Message of George Fox.* Richmond, IN: Friends United Press, 1984.

Hamm, Thomas D. *The Transformation of American Quakerism: Orthodox Friends, 1800-1907.* Bloomington, IN: Indiana University Press, 1988.

Ingle, H. Larry. *Quakers in Conflict: The Hicksite Reformation.* Knoxville, TN: University of Tennessee Press, 1986.

Janney, S. M. *Conversations on Religious Subjects, Between a Father and His Sons.* Philadelphia: Friends' Publication Association, 1868.

Jones, Rufus M. *The Faith and Practice of the Quakers.* Richmond, IN: Friends United Press, 1989.

Jones, T. Canby, ed. *"The Power of the Lord Is Over All": The Pastoral Letters of George Fox.* Richmond, IN: Friends United Press, 1989.

Kenworthy, Leonard B. *Quakerism: A Study Guide on the Religious Society of Friends.* Dublin, IN: Prinit Press, 1981.

————, ed. *Quaker Quotations on Faith and Practice.* Philadelphia: Friends General Conference and Quaker Publications, 1983.

King, Rachel Hadley. *George Fox and the Light Within, 1650-1660.* Philadelphia: Friends Book Store, 1940.

Loukes, Harold. *The Quaker Contribution.* London: SCM Press, 1965.

Peck, George T. *What Is Quakerism? A Primer.* Pamphlet No. 277. Wallingford, PA: Pendle Hill Publication, 1988.

Principles of Quakerism: A Collection of Essays. Philadelphia: Issued by Representatives of the Religious Society of Friends for Pennsylvania, New Jersey, and Delaware, 1908.

Punshon, John. *Alternative Christianity.* Pamphlet No. 245. Wallingford, PA: Pendle Hill Publication, 1982.

————, *Letter To A Universalist.* Pamphlet No. 285. Wallingford, PA: Pendle Hill Publication, 1989.

_____, *Portrait in Grey: A Short History of the Quakers*. London: Quaker Home Service, 1984.

Trueblood, D. Elton. *The People Called Quakers*. New York: Harper & Row, 1966.

Scott, Janet. *What Canst Thou Say? Toward a Quaker Theology*. Swarthmore Lecture 1980. London: Quaker Home Service, 1980.

Ullmann, Richard K. *Friends And Truth*. London: Friends Home Service Committee, 1955.

Willcuts, Jack L. *A Family of Friends: Friends Church Membership Course*. Newberg, OR: The Barclay Press, 1977.

_____. *Why Friends Are Friends: Some Quaker Core Convictions*. Newberg, OR: The Barclay Press, 1984.

Williams, Walter R. *The Rich Heritage of Quakerism*. ed. by Paul Anderson. Newberg, OR: The Barclay Press, 1987.

Quaker Periodicals

The Canadian Friend. CYM Office, 91A Fourth Avenue, Ottawa, Canada
   K1S 2L1

The Friend (London). Drayton House, 30 Gordon Street, London, England
   WC1H OBQ

Friends Journal. 1501 Cherry Street, Philadelphia, PA 19102

Friends Quarterly. 136 Wellington Road, Manchester, England M14 6AR

The Journal of The Friends Historical Society (London). The Library, Friends
   House, Euston Road, London, England NW1 2BJ

Quaker History. (Formerly *Bulletin of Friends Historical Association*) Quaker
   collection, Haverford College, Haverford, PA 19041

Quaker Life. 101 Quaker Hill Drive, Richmond, IN 47374

Quaker Religious Thought. c/o Phil Smith, Religion Dept., George Fox
   University, Newberg, OR 97132

The Southern Friend. The Library, Guilford College, 5600 Friendly Avenue,
   Greensboro, NC 27410

Index

F

Scripture Index

New Testament _____